DO YOU REALLY WANT

The majority of the deals in this book, says Terence Reese in his Foreword, are derived from *Bridge: 66 curiosités* by the famous Swiss players, Jean Besse and Pierre Béguin, both masters of rubber bridge as well as of the tournament game.

Many cherished notions, such as the importance of of finding a 4–4 fit and the merits of standard leads, are blown to the winds. There are many unfamiliar and lethally brilliant ideas, too, in the field of declarer's play.

When you have read this book you could be not just a better player, but a top player.

Also by Terence Reese

BRIDGE FOR AMBITIOUS PLAYERS

Mini-Masters
MASTER PLAYS IN A SINGLE SUIT
MASTER DECEPTIVE PLAYS

with José Le Dentu
BRIDGE: TRIUMPHS AND DISASTERS

with Roger Trézel
BLOCKING AND UNBLOCKING PLAYS IN BRIDGE
SAFETY PLAYS IN BRIDGE
ELIMINATION PLAYS IN BRIDGE
SNARES AND SWINDLES IN BRIDGE
THOSE EXTRA CHANCES IN BRIDGE
WHEN TO DUCK, WHEN TO WIN IN BRIDGE
MASTER THE ODDS IN BRIDGE
THE ART OF DEFENCE IN BRIDGE
THE MISTAKES YOU MAKE AT BRIDGE

with Rixi Markus
BETTER BRIDGE FOR CLUB PLAYERS

with David Bird
MIRACLES OF CARD PLAY
UNHOLY TRICKS: More Miraculous Card Play
DOUBLED AND VENERABLE: Further Miracles of Card Play
BRIDGE — TRICKS OF THE TRADE

with Julian Pottage
POSITIVE DEFENCE
POSITIVE DECLARER'S PLAY

Do You Really Want to Win at Bridge?

TERENCE REESE

LONDON
VICTOR GOLLANCZ LTD
in association with
PETER CRAWLEY
1991

First published in Great Britain in February 1989
in association with Peter Crawley
by Victor Gollancz Ltd,
14 Henrietta Street, London WC2E 8QJ
Second impression January 1991

British Library Cataloguing in Publication Data
Reese, Terence
  Do you really want to win at bridge? —
  (Master bridge series).
  1. Contract bridge — Questions & answers
  I. Title II. Besse, Jean III. Béguin, Pierre, *1913*-
  V. Bridge 66 Curiosités. *English*
  795.41'5'076

  ISBN 0-575-04404-7

Original French version published in 1987
         by Journal de Genève
      as *BRIDGE: 66 CURIOSITÉS*
      by Pierre Béguin & Jean Besse

Photoset and printed by WBC Print Ltd, Bridgend

Contents

Foreword

The majority of the deals in this book are derived from *Bridge: 66 curiosités'* by the famous Swiss players, Jean Besse and Pierre Béguin, published under the auspices of the *Journal de Genève*. Both are masters of rubber bridge as well as of the tournament game, and this has provided them with various insights not found in British or American books.

Books consisting of individual deals have been common lately—I have contributed my share. The special quality of this one is that all the deals—well, almost all—are *instructive*: they describe types of bidding and play that often occur but are not the material of the average text-book.

Jean Besse writes for the *Journal de Genève*. His quizzical expression has been a familiar sight at all the big tournaments for forty years. He must have more friends and acquaintances than any *bridgeur* in Europe. In addition to being an outstanding player and theorist, he serves on many international committees, bringing to these bodies a rare injection of commonsense.

Pierre Béguin has been correspondent of the *Gazette de Lausanne* since 1949. He founded the Swiss Bridge League and was its first playing captain. A special brand of humour lies behind a somewhat austere manner. I remember driving with him to the championship at Montreux in 1954. He pointed to a distant area of the countryside and said: 'In the war I used to patrol that border, alone on horseback. My orders were to report, and repel, any German invasion.'

1

The Angry Brigade

Quite a storm blew up when this deal was played in the weekly duplicate at the club.

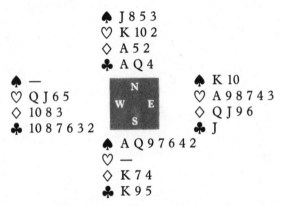

```
              ♠ J 8 5 3
              ♡ K 10 2
              ◇ A 5 2
              ♣ A Q 4
  ♠ —                        ♠ K 10
  ♡ Q J 6 5                  ♡ A 9 8 7 4 3
  ◇ 10 8 3                   ◇ Q J 9 6
  ♣ 10 8 7 6 3 2             ♣ J
              ♠ A Q 9 7 6 4 2
              ♡ —
              ◇ K 7 4
              ♣ K 9 5
```

East was the dealer at love all. South became the declarer in six spades after this sequence:

South	West	North	East
—	—	—	1♡
2♠(1)	No	4♠	No
4NT(2)	No	5♡	No
6♠	No	No	No

(1) The hand may seem strong for a jump overcall, but it is not so powerful unless there are entries to the opposite hand.

(2) It is unusual to follow a limit bid with a slam try, but the South hand looks very different after the double raise.

West led the queen of hearts and the declarer quite rightly played low from dummy. He ruffed and crossed to the ace of clubs, noting the fall of the jack. Then he led the jack of spades from the table.

When East followed unemotionally with the 10 South consulted the ceiling and finally, with a learned air, played low. When the jack held, he announced proudly, 'I draw the ace of spades and claim twelve tricks.'

Instead of looking pleased, North exclaimed angrily, 'Why don't you play on? With all those menace cards there must be an excellent chance of an overtrick and a likely top!'

'How could I make seven?' South replied. 'The diamonds were Axx opposite Kxx and there was no chance of a squeeze.'

'Of course there was a squeeze', said North, who had had time to study the cards. 'A double trump squeeze, actually. After the play to the first trick you can place West with the jack of hearts and East with the ace. This is the end position:

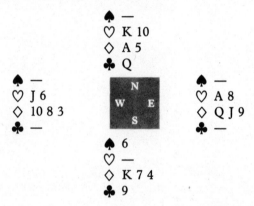

♠ —
♡ K 10
◇ A 5
♣ Q

♠ —
♡ J 6
◇ 10 8 3
♣ —

♠ —
♡ A 8
◇ Q J 9
♣ —

♠ 6
♡ —
◇ K 7 4
♣ 9

'Now you cross to the queen of clubs in dummy. West cannot bare the jack of hearts, so he throws a diamond. Then East is squeezed. Any fool can see that. And you didn't even try!'

2

False Picture

Sometimes you will arrive at your final contract without having unmasked all your batteries. On such occasions it may be wiser to play a deceptive game than to seek a remote technical solution. Two examples follow, the first from rubber bridge at Crans-sur-Sierre.

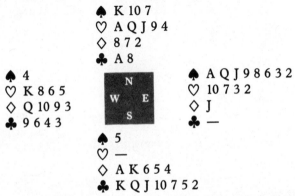

```
                ♠ K 10 7
                ♡ A Q J 9 4
                ◇ 8 7 2
                ♣ A 8
  ♠ 4                            ♠ A Q J 9 8 6 3 2
  ♡ K 8 6 5          N           ♡ 10 7 3 2
  ◇ Q 10 9 3     W       E       ◇ J
  ♣ 9 6 4 3          S           ♣ —
                ♠ 5
                ♡ —
                ◇ A K 6 5 4
                ♣ K Q J 10 7 5 2
```

At love all North opened one heart and East overcalled with four spades. South made the sensible call—six clubs—and all passed.

West led a spade to the queen and East returned a low spade. South ruffed high and West discarded a diamond.

There is just one technical possibility. South may dream of finessing the 8 of clubs, then playing ace and queen of hearts. If East has the king of hearts, and if the 10 comes down in three rounds, and if the clubs are 2–2 . . .

South was a good enough player to see all this in a few seconds, but he was also shrewd enough to form a different plan. He played off six more rounds of trumps. West, fearing that South might hold a singleton heart, clung to three hearts and two diamonds. East, rather foolishly, retained his four hearts instead of playing an early high–low to assist his partner. At the finish South led the ace of diamonds and bashfully claimed the remainder when all followed.

For various reasons it wasn't clever of the defenders to cling to their heart holdings. South would hardly have leapt to six clubs if he had been missing three aces. And if South *had* held 1-1-4-7 shape, West would in any event have been squeezed in the red suits.

A deal with a rather similar point occurred at a club in Geneva:

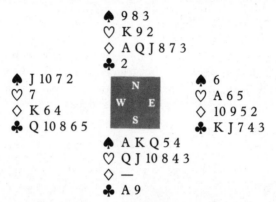

```
                    ♠ 9 8 3
                    ♡ K 9 2
                    ◇ A Q J 8 7 3
                    ♣ 2
  ♠ J 10 7 2                        ♠ 6
  ♡ 7                               ♡ A 6 5
  ◇ K 6 4                           ◇ 10 9 5 2
  ♣ Q 10 8 6 5                      ♣ K J 7 4 3
                    ♠ A K Q 5 4
                    ♡ Q J 10 8 4 3
                    ◇ —
                    ♣ A 9
```

South opened one heart at game all. It may seem natural for North to respond two diamonds, but as the partners were playing five-card majors North, eager to end the rubber, raised directly to four hearts. South bid 5 NT—Josephine (Culbertson), asking partner to bid seven if he held two of the three top honours in hearts. North could bid only six hearts and West led his singleton trump.

East won with the ace of hearts and returned his singleton spade, won by the ace. The declarer took a club ruff, drew a second round of trumps, then led a spade from the table. East ruffed and South said feebly, 'I was making the normal safety play in case the hand with four spades did not hold a trump.'

What do you think of that excuse? If West had held a singleton spade in addition to his known singleton in hearts he would not have led a trump, abandoning all hope of a ruff.

It would have been much better play for the declarer to take the club ruff and play off all the hearts. West might have been foolish enough to unguard spades in order to keep K x x in diamonds. West should remember that South had made a grand slam try of 5 NT, so could hardly hold a losing diamond. But then, you don't win any medals at this game by expecting opponents always to play well.

3

The Redouble by Responder (1)

Your partner opens with a bid at the one level and second hand doubles. What is your plan now? When do you pass, bid a new suit, or redouble?

It is a big subject and one where fashions have changed many times during the life of contract bridge. The most popular style nowadays is as follows:

—Pass when you have nothing to say.

—Bid naturally with a moderate hand. A simple change of suit is not forcing (but even here there are variations in practice).

—Redouble with a strong hand.

—A jump in a new suit (one heart—double—three clubs) used to be played as forcing for one round but nowadays is more often pre-emptive.

Note that a redouble does not necessarily express strong support for partner's suit. On the contrary, if partner has opened one spade and the second player doubles, a redouble is an excellent move on a 10-point 1–4–4–4 type.

It is sometimes said that a redouble is always penalty-oriented, but that is not necessarily so. Consider this type, after partner has opened one heart:

♠ 8 4 2
♡ A K 5
♢ A J 3
♣ 8 7 4 2

If the next player doubles, neither two hearts nor three hearts is appropriate. For the moment, you must redouble. Suppose now that the bidding develops as follows:

South	West	North	East
1♡	Dble	Redble	No
No	1♠	?	

Now two hearts would not be a crime and three hearts would not lead to disaster. Just pass! This, following your redouble, is certainly forcing. When one spade comes round to South he bids two diamonds. West retires from the fray. What should North bid now?

Well, it would be feeble to bid only three hearts, on the grounds that you had no shape and had already shown values by redoubling. You can be sure that your partner has shape, so your 4–3–3–3 distribution no longer matters. Also, the fact that South passed on the second round, following the redouble, means that he does not hold a minimum two-suiter. With excellent support for both partner's suits, North can surely go to four hearts.

Now we are going to change the bowling and consider a defensive problem, as seen by West.

                    ♠ 8 4 2
                    ♡ A K 5
                    ◇ A J 3
                    ♣ 8 7 4 2
    ♠ A Q 10 3
    ♡ 8 7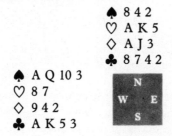
    ◇ 9 4 2
    ♣ A K 5 3

The bidding has followed the line suggested above:

South	West	North	East
1♡	Dble	Redble	No
No	1♠	No	No
2◇	No	4♡	No
No	No		

West leads the king (or ace) of clubs, East plays the queen and declarer the 6. What should West play now? Consider your answer, then look at the next page.

4

The Redouble by Responder (2)

To restate the problem: the bidding has been:

South	West	North	East
1♡	Dble	Redble	No
No	1♠	No	No
2♢	No	4♡	No
No	No		

West leads the king of clubs and the dummy goes down:

```
              ♠ 8 4 2
              ♡ A K 5
              ♢ A J 3
              ♣ 8 7 4 2
  ♠ A Q 10 3       N
  ♡ 8 7       W        E
  ♢ 9 4 2          S
  ♣ A K 5 3
```

East plays the queen of clubs and declarer the 6. What should West play now?

Did you, by any mischance, say to yourself: 'I play a low club, of course. Partner is marked with the jack and I want him to be in to lead a spade.'

Don't despair. Ninety-nine players out of every hundred would do the same. But it's wrong.

If South is 5–4 in the red suits, as seems likely from the bidding, there can be no hurry to lead a low club. You can do that later. But suppose South has a singleton club (much more likely than a singleton spade). The full hand might well be something like this:

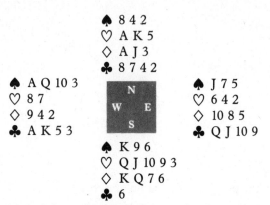

```
              ♠ 8 4 2
              ♡ A K 5
              ◇ A J 3
              ♣ 8 7 4 2
♠ A Q 10 3                    ♠ J 7 5
♡ 8 7          N              ♡ 6 4 2
◇ 9 4 2     W     E           ◇ 10 8 5
♣ A K 5 3      S              ♣ Q J 10 9
              ♠ K 9 6
              ♡ Q J 10 9 3
              ◇ K Q 7 6
              ♣ 6
```

So another club won't be fatal, did you say? But it will! South will be happy to accept the force and play on reverse dummy lines: ruff the club, queen and another heart, club ruff, diamond to the ace and club ruff. This leaves:

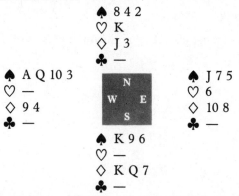

```
              ♠ 8 4 2
              ♡ K
              ◇ J 3
              ♣ —
♠ A Q 10 3                    ♠ J 7 5
♡ —            N              ♡ 6
◇ 9 4      W     E            ◇ 10 8
♣ —            S              ♣ —
              ♠ K 9 6
              ♡ —
              ◇ K Q 7
              ♣ —
```

South crosses to ◇ J, draws the outstanding trump, and makes two more tricks in diamonds, ten in all.

To defeat this line of play West must lead a trump at trick two. This is normally the best defence when the declarer threatens to play a crossruff or a reverse dummy (which is a form of crossruff).

One other point is worth mentioning. Suppose South's spades had been as good as K J x: can he then make four hearts after the trump switch at trick two? He can, if he does everything right: club lead, trump switch won in dummy, club ruff, diamond to ace, club ruff, diamond to jack, club ruff; now king of diamonds, heart queen, and king of spades, taken by the ace, leaves West on play.

5

Averting a Crisscross

The last deal showed how to defend against a reverse dummy. This one describes a form of defence against a special type of squeeze. A Swiss woman international did the wrong thing at the table. She says it will never happen again.

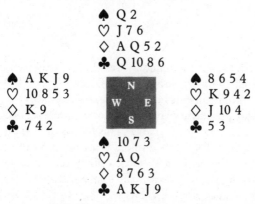

```
              ♠ Q 2
              ♡ J 7 6
              ◇ A Q 5 2
              ♣ Q 10 8 6
♠ A K J 9                      ♠ 8 6 5 4
♡ 10 8 5 3        N            ♡ K 9 4 2
◇ K 9         W       E        ◇ J 10 4
♣ 7 4 2           S            ♣ 5 3
              ♠ 10 7 3
              ♡ A Q
              ◇ 8 7 6 3
              ♣ A K J 9
```

On the first hand of a rubber the bidding followed this optimistic course:

South	North
1♣	1◇
2◇	3♣
3NT	No

West (the anti-heroine of our story) led the king of spades and her partner signalled with the 6. Confident that this was the beginning of an echo to show four cards, West followed with the ace of spades, then the jack and the 9. With four tricks in the bag, she coyly placed the 9 of diamonds on the table. (Note that this could hardly cost, because if the declarer held such as Jxxx he would presumably lead low to the queen and bring down the king on the next round.)

South, needless to say, was in no position to decline the diamond finesse. When the queen held he finessed the queen of hearts, then played on clubs, arriving at this endgame:

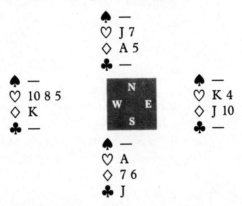

On the jack of clubs a diamond was thrown from dummy and East was caught in a crisscross squeeze.

There are three elements in every squeeze—menaces, entries and timing. As any proficient player knows, most squeezes occur when all the tricks but one are available. This means that when you are defending against 3NT you do not, as a rule, want to create the position where the declarer has lost exactly four tricks. It was a mistake, in other words, to cash the four spades.

Indeed, it would even be a mistake here to cash *three* spades. Suppose that West begins with ♠ A K J and then, knowing a little about the defence to squeeze play, switches to a heart. South wins, cashes three clubs, and finesses ◊ Q. The position is now:

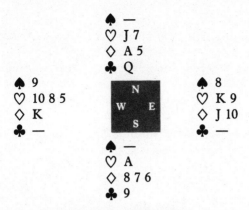

                    ♠ —
                    ♡ J 7
                    ◊ A 5
                    ♣ Q

    ♠ 9   ♠ 8
    ♡ 10 8 5   N   ♡ K 9
    ◊ K   W   E   ◊ J 10
    ♣ —   S   ♣ —

                    ♠ —
                    ♡ A
                    ◊ 8 7 6
                    ♣ 9

On the last club East must part with the 8 of spades. Then ace and another diamond spells his doom.

So it comes to this: after just two rounds of spades West does best to switch to a heart. And if South exits with a spade, hoping to improve his timing, West plays a second heart, removing the threat in this suit.

6

At the Olympiad

In the 1972 Olympiad at Miami the Swiss team scored a 17–3 victory against the great Italian team that won the event. This was a fine result for Switzerland:

Dealer South   Game all

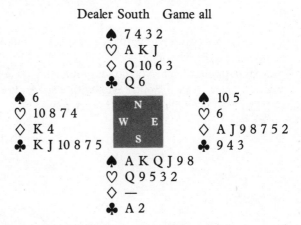

```
                  ♠ 7 4 3 2
                  ♡ A K J
                  ◇ Q 10 6 3
                  ♣ Q 6
♠ 6                                    ♠ 10 5
♡ 10 8 7 4            N                ♡ 6
◇ K 4          W           E           ◇ A J 9 8 7 5 2
♣ K J 10 8 7 5       S                 ♣ 9 4 3
                  ♠ A K Q J 9 8
                  ♡ Q 9 5 3 2
                  ◇ —
                  ♣ A 2
```

In the closed room Forquet and Garozzo were playing the Precision system. This was their sequence:

South	North
Garozzo	Forquet
1♣	1NT(1)
2♡(2)	3◇(3)
3♠	4♡(4)
4NT	5♡
6♡	No

(1) Showing the high cards in terms of 2 for an ace, 1 for a king.

(2) After the positive response this showed a suit but was also an asking bid in hearts.

(3) Indicating the high cards in hearts.

(4) Forquet, evidently, did not regard South's three spades as a genuine, and possibly longer, suit.

In hearts only twelve tricks could be made: 1430 to Italy.

The bidding at the other table was—interesting.

South	West	North	East
Besse	Avarelli	Fenwick	Belladonna
2♣	No	2♡(1)	3♢(2)
3♠	No	4♡(3)	No
5NT(4)	No	7♠(5)	No
No	No		

(1) This, in the continental style, showed the ace of a red suit.

(2) You don't easily keep Giorgio quiet.

(3) North was rather awkwardly placed at this point. He has spade support and perhaps five hearts would have been a possibility, to indicate the additional controls in this suit. Four hearts was theoretically natural, but North was confident that the bidding would not die.

(4) The grand slam force, asking partner to bid seven with two of the three top honours.

(5) But Fenwick knew that spades were the real destination.

In seven spades there was no problem. South ruffed the diamond lead, drew trumps, and discarded dummy's club loser on the long hearts. That was 2210 to North–South and a swing of 13 international match points to Switzerland.

7

Short Story

Timing, tempo, rhythm of play? Call it what you will, this element of the game is difficult to analyse or define. Study this example from the European Championship at Lausanne:

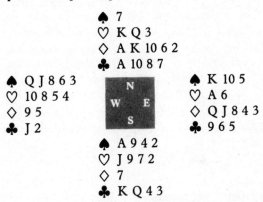

```
                  ♠ 7
                  ♡ K Q 3
                  ◊ A K 10 6 2
                  ♣ A 10 8 7
  ♠ Q J 8 6 3                      ♠ K 10 5
  ♡ 10 8 5 4                       ♡ A 6
  ◊ 9 5                            ◊ Q J 8 4 3
  ♣ J 2                            ♣ 9 6 5
                  ♠ A 9 4 2
                  ♡ J 9 7 2
                  ◊ 7
                  ♣ K Q 4 3
```

East was the dealer and North–South were vulnerable. Five clubs, 3 NT and four hearts are all possible contracts for North–South. In the match between Denmark and the Netherlands both teams attempted four hearts. This was the bidding by the Dutch pair:

South	West	North	East
—	—	—	No
No	No	1♣(1)	1♠(2)
No	2♠	Dble	No
3♠	No	4◊	No
4♡	No	No(3)	No

(1) Precision, normally 16 points upwards.
(2) Players defending against a conventional one club often

devise special defensive systems, especially by a passed player. Here one spade denoted at least three spades and not more than two hearts.

(3) There was a strong inference that South held only four hearts and it might have been wise for North to transfer to five clubs. Hands with a 4-3 trump fit are always awkward to manage when the shorter hand holds two high trumps.

The Dutch South was Toine van Hoof, a name reminiscent of a Somerset Maugham short story. When West led a low spade to the king South made a clever play: he allowed the king to hold. The spade return was ruffed in dummy, the king of hearts lost to the ace, and on a third round of spades South produced the ace. Then came a heart to dummy, a club to the king, jack of hearts and two rounds of diamonds, on which the fourth spade went away. The defenders made just two hearts and one spade.

At the other table the jack of clubs was led against four hearts. The Danish declarer took the trick and led a heart to the queen and ace. When East returned a club, South won and took a spade ruff. Another spade went on the second round of diamonds, but now South was awkwardly placed, as these were the remaining cards:

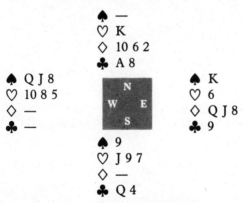

```
                    ♠ —
                    ♡ K
                    ◇ 10 6 2
                    ♣ A 8
        ♠ Q J 8         N         ♠ K
        ♡ 10 8 5                  ♡ 6
        ◇ —       W       E       ◇ Q J 8
        ♣ —           S           ♣ 9
                    ♠ 9
                    ♡ J 9 7
                    ◇ —
                    ♣ Q 4
```

After cashing the king of hearts South led a club to the queen. West ruffed, put his partner in with the king of spades, and made another trump trick when East led a diamond.

How do you think that South should have played after the club lead? His best play is to follow the line adopted by the declarer at the other table. Begin with a *low* spade from hand. This keeps everything under control, as one of the remaining spades can be ruffed and one goes away on the high diamond.

8

On Guard

It is not difficult to reach the grand slam in hearts on the deal below. Playing the Acol system, South may open two hearts, forcing for one round. North responds two spades and South bids four hearts, promising a solid suit. North will bid 4NT, the 'old Black', and proceed to seven hearts when his partner admits to two aces.

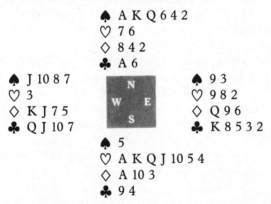

```
              ♠ A K Q 6 4 2
              ♡ 7 6
              ◇ 8 4 2
              ♣ A 6
♠ J 10 8 7                      ♠ 9 3
♡ 3             N               ♡ 9 8 2
◇ K J 7 5    W     E            ◇ Q 9 6
♣ Q J 10 7        S            ♣ K 8 5 3 2
              ♠ 5
              ♡ A K Q J 10 5 4
              ◇ A 10 3
              ♣ 9 4
```

West leads the queen of clubs and two questions arise:

1. How should South play to make his grand slam against any defence?

2. Suppose that South can see only the dummy's cards and his own: can he then reasonably make thirteen tricks?

We will look first at the problem with open cards. It is not particularly difficult even if the endgame is not foreseen from the first. South wins with the ace of clubs and plays six rounds of hearts, discarding two spades (only one long card is needed) and two diamonds from the dummy. He arrives at this position:

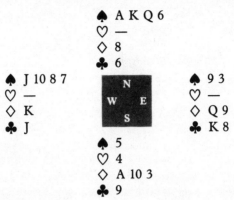

```
                    ♠ A K Q 6
                    ♡ —
                    ◇ 8
                    ♣ 6
  ♠ J 10 8 7                          ♠ 9 3
  ♡ —                                 ♡ —
  ◇ K                                 ◇ Q 9
  ♣ J                                 ♣ K 8
                    ♠ 5
                    ♡ 4
                    ◇ A 10 3
                    ♣ 9
```

On the last trump West certainly cannot let go a spade. If he throws the jack of clubs, then three rounds of spades will expose East to a squeeze in the minor suits. West's best bet, therefore, appears to be the king of diamonds. Declarer discards a club from the table, cashes three spades, and then, with A 10 of diamonds over East's Q 9, he takes the finesse.

Why should he finesse? Well, for one thing West would have preferred a diamond lead had he held K Q J. For another, West's last card, apart from the spades, is surely the jack of clubs. (True, a more accomplished defender would have thrown this card at an earlier stage, since it was 'a card he was known to hold'.)

The play is called a 'guard squeeze', because West was unable to retain the king of diamonds, which would have protected his partner from the finesse.

Now let's consider the situation when South cannot see the opposing cards. All he will know, after the opening lead, is that West is likely to hold the jack of clubs and East the king. As before, he begins with the ace of clubs and seven rounds of hearts, keeping these cards:

♠ A K Q 6
♡ —
♢ 8
♣ —

♠ 5
♡ —
♢ A 10 3
♣ 9

He takes three rounds of spades, keeping a careful eye on East's play. On the second spade he himself discards the 3 of diamonds; and then, if the 9 of clubs is not a master, he throws his club. By this time he knows that West began with four spades and also that West, on the long hearts, has parted with the king and jack of diamonds. (As we saw earlier, this is West's best defence.) The situation is much the same as before: a finesse of the 10 of diamonds is virtually certain to succeed.

9

The Weak and the Strong

Suppose that the deal below were to occur in a 7-table pairs event. The contract at every table, it is charitable to assume, would be four spades by South. My estimate is that in a game of average standard five declarers would go one down; but the *weakest* and the *strongest* would make the contract.

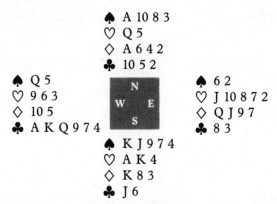

A simple auction—not that simple auctions are common these days—might go like this:

South	West	North	East
1♠	2♣	3♠	No
4♠	No	No	No

West begins with three rounds of clubs; East discards a heart and South ruffs.

Now you know what the majority would do. Knowing that in terms of probability there was not much to choose between a 3–1 and a 2–2 break of four outstanding cards, they would lead a spade to the ace and finesse on the way back. Later they would lose a trick in diamonds and finish one down.

'Sorry, partner. As the clubs were 6–2 I think I was right to play West for the singleton spade.'

At one of the seven tables Mrs Guggenheim holds the South cards. Mindful of the old slogan, 'Eight ever, nine never', she bangs out ace and king of spades and makes the contract.

Now, what happens when the club expert plays this contract of four spades? Beginners are told to draw trumps unless they plan to ruff in the short hand or to crossruff, but good players seldom do this when there is any problem about the trump situation. When possible, they aim to get more information before they tackle the suit.

On the present occasion, therefore, South ruffs the third club, then cashes king of diamonds and two rounds of hearts. So far, an adverse ruff is extremely unlikely. A third heart is led and West, as it happens, follows suit. It would not matter if he ruffed or discarded.

The next move is another diamond from hand. If West ruffs he will be ruffing a loser, so there is no risk in this play. The ace wins, and as it is now impossible for West to hold three spades the next move is to cash dummy's ace of spades. This leaves:

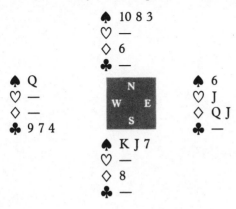

[29]

No more inspired (apparently) than the other declarers, South runs the 8 of spades, losing to the queen. But now the luckless West is compelled to concede a ruff-and-discard.

You see, the most important thing at this game is to be able to count to thirteen.

10

Not Many, But Much

It is interesting that some countries with a tiny bridge-playing population have done remarkably well in international events. Pakistan, for example, has often been prominent in world play, Chinese Taipei (Taiwan) has twice been in the last four. This is a deal from the 1979 Bermuda Bowl:

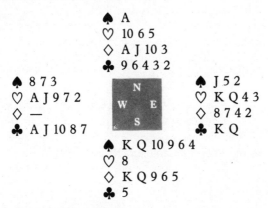

```
                    ♠ A
                    ♡ 10 6 5
                    ◇ A J 10 3
                    ♣ 9 6 4 3 2
  ♠ 8 7 3                          ♠ J 5 2
  ♡ A J 9 7 2          N           ♡ K Q 4 3
  ◇ —               W     E        ◇ 8 7 4 2
  ♣ A J 10 8 7          S          ♣ K Q
                    ♠ K Q 10 9 6 4
                    ♡ 8
                    ◇ K Q 9 6 5
                    ♣ 5
```

West was the dealer at game all and this was the bidding between Taipei and the United States:

South	West	North	East
Brachman	Kuo	Passell	Huang
—	1♡	No	3♡
4♠(1)	No	No	Dble(2)
No	No	No(3)	

(1) Intrepid.
(2) This seems a trifle quaint. I don't see that he had much defence against spades. Perhaps he regarded the sequence as forcing.

(3) Passell must have been surprised, with two aces and not having entered the bidding; but one doesn't redouble on these occasions.

I dare say that even without his partner's double West might have underled the ace of hearts. He chose the 9, indicating that he looked for a return of the higher suit as between diamonds and clubs. So Huang, when he won with the queen of hearts, returned a diamond for his partner to ruff. This time, the 2 proclaimed an entry in clubs. West underled an ace for the second time and ruffed the next diamond to defeat the contract.

This sparkling defence was not highly rewarded. At the other table the American East–West, Kantar and Eisenberg, climbed to five hearts over four spades. North–South doubled, naturally, but owing to the blockage in spades they were unable to take the three tricks that belonged to them. Indeed, it looks as though West can make twelve tricks even if North switches to a trump at trick two. When South shows out on the second round of hearts West can safely play K Q of clubs. Then he ruffs a diamond, discards two spades on high clubs, and makes the rest of the tricks with a crossruff.

In the other matches of the qualifying round, Brazil v Panama and Italy v Australia, one West was allowed to play in four hearts and three South players made game in spades, their opponents not finding the defence of Huang and Kuo.

11

Four-headed Monster

The remarkable deal below was played at rubber bridge by Tony Trad, winner of numerous events in Egypt and later a Swiss international.

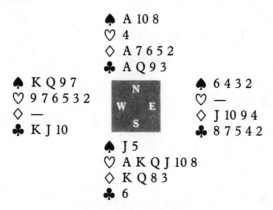

```
              ♠ A 10 8
              ♡ 4
              ◇ A 7 6 5 2
              ♣ A Q 9 3
  ♠ K Q 9 7                    ♠ 6 4 3 2
  ♡ 9 7 6 5 3 2                ♡ —
  ◇ —                          ◇ J 10 9 4
  ♣ K J 10                     ♣ 8 7 5 4 2
              ♠ J 5
              ♡ A K Q J 10 8
              ◇ K Q 8 3
              ♣ 6
```

South was the dealer at game all and the bidding went like this:

South	North
1♡	2◇
4NT(1)	5♠(2)
7NT(3)	No

(1) Not classical, but the sort of bid a good player will make at rubber bridge with a less skilful partner. If North has one ace, South will take a chance in five diamonds; if two aces, in six diamonds. Spades may not be led or partner may hold the king.

(2) Showing three aces in the traditional manner. In tournament play it is more usual to respond five clubs with 0 or 3 aces, five diamonds with 1 or 4.

(3) If partner has five diamonds there will probably be thirteen tricks on top; if only four, he will probably hold some additional value or there may be a squeeze.

This analysis looked fine when West led the king of spades and the dummy went down. But there were terrible shocks: West showed out on the first round of diamonds, East on the first round of hearts.

The thirteen expected winners were now down to ten; eleven if you assume that the club finesse will win. Still a long way from home. After ace of spades, two top diamonds and four top hearts, the position was:

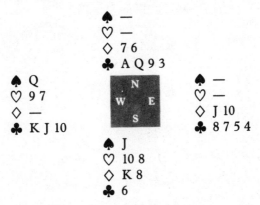

```
              ♠ —
              ♡ —
              ◇ 7 6
              ♣ A Q 9 3
♠ Q                          ♠ —
♡ 9 7          N             ♡ —
◇ —        W       E         ◇ J 10
♣ K J 10       S             ♣ 8 7 5 4
              ♠ J
              ♡ 10 8
              ◇ K 8
              ♣ 6
```

The strange thing now is that all four suits are guarded by the defence. Also, East controls the fourth round of clubs.

But not for long. When Trad led the 10 of hearts, discarding a diamond from dummy, East had to throw a club, trusting that his partner would be able to control the third round. But now the king of diamonds was the start of a progressive squeeze against West.

Have you ever seen at the table a squeeze position in which there were menace cards in four suits? I know I haven't.

12

Sensible System

Suppose that North and South hold:

♠ A 6 3
♥ 8 7 6 2
♦ K 6
♣ K Q 10 5

♠ K J 9 5 2
♥ Q 3
♦ A Q J 9 4
♣ J

The bidding begins:

South	North
1♠	2♣
2♦	?

What do you think North should say now? I know what most tournament players would bid: two hearts, the precious fourth suit. This would turn out all right on the present occasion, because South would bid two spades, limiting his hand, and North would then settle for four spades.

Nevertheless, I think that these fourth suit bids are much overdone. The answer chosen by North on the actual deal may surprise you.

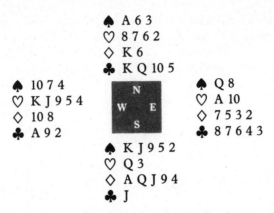

```
              ♠ A 6 3
              ♡ 8 7 6 2
              ◇ K 6
              ♣ K Q 10 5
♠ 10 7 4          N          ♠ Q 8
♡ K J 9 5 4   W     E        ♡ A 10
◇ 10 8            S          ◇ 7 5 3 2
♣ A 9 2                      ♣ 8 7 6 4 3
              ♠ K J 9 5 2
              ♡ Q 3
              ◇ A Q J 9 4
              ♣ J
```

Over South's two diamonds North bid simply *two* spades. In what may be called old-fashioned Acol this would not have been forcing. In the modern world responses at the level of two always promise fair values, and there is much to be said for treating them as forcing to 2NT. I won't go into a sideways discussion now, but there are many occasions when such an understanding is useful.

Against the eventual four spades West led a heart to the ace and East returned the 10. West won and played a third heart, which East correctly ruffed with the queen. South overruffed and suffered the ignominy of going one down, as he still had to lose a trump and a club.

This was poor play by both sides, as I dare say you will have realised. When East ruffed with the queen of spades South should have discarded his jack of clubs, playing loser on loser in approved fashion. That is elementary, and the main interest lies in the earlier defence. West must cash the ace of clubs before leading the third round of hearts.

Knowing that his partner would always do the wrong thing if given the opportunity, East took the blame. 'I should have led something like the 7 of clubs at trick two,' he said. 'You make the ace of clubs, play king and another heart. We make a fourth trick via the trump promotion.' West nodded sagely.

To lead a club at trick two, nursing partner, would have been good tactics here, but it might possibly have been wrong—for example, if South had held Q x x of hearts and a void club. Then the winning defence would have been to make three tricks in hearts and play a fourth round for the trump promotion. But no doubt West, after making three hearts, would have tried to cash the ace of clubs!

13

Test Match

Suppose that you had to play 3 NT on these cards, against the lead of a low spade, which runs conveniently to the 10.

$$
\begin{array}{ll}
& \spadesuit\ 9\ 8 \\
& \heartsuit\ K\ J\ 3 \\
& \diamondsuit\ K\ 7\ 5\ 2 \\
& \clubsuit\ Q\ 10\ 6\ 3 \\
\end{array}
$$

$\spadesuit$ 6 led

$$
\begin{array}{ll}
& \spadesuit\ A\ K\ 10 \\
& \heartsuit\ A\ 10\ 8\ 5 \\
& \diamondsuit\ 8\ 6 \\
& \clubsuit\ A\ J\ 9\ 5 \\
\end{array}
$$

The deal occurred in a match between two strong American teams. At both tables South had opened 1 NT (not my choice, with a plain doubleton and this kind of texture) and North had raised to 3 NT.

After winning with $\spadesuit$ 10 both declarers crossed to the king of hearts and finessed in clubs, running the 10 and losing to the king. At one table West switched to queen and another diamond. The contract was safe now, because this was the full hand:

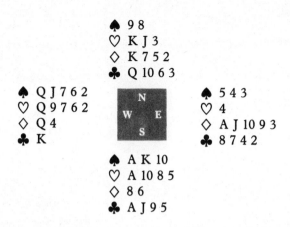

```
                    ♠ 9 8
                    ♡ K J 3
                    ◇ K 7 5 2
                    ♣ Q 10 6 3
♠ Q J 7 6 2                        ♠ 5 4 3
♡ Q 9 7 6 2         N              ♡ 4
◇ Q 4           W       E          ◇ A J 10 9 3
♣ K                 S              ♣ 8 7 4 2
                    ♠ A K 10
                    ♡ A 10 8 5
                    ◇ 8 6
                    ♣ A J 9 5
```

When East won the second round of diamonds there was nothing he could do to prevent the declarer from establishing a ninth trick. On the neutral return of a spade, for example, South will lose a heart trick to the safe hand, West, but that will be all.

West's lead of the queen of diamonds, when in with the king of clubs, seemed at the time to be clever play, but the other defender saw more deeply into the position. He played a second round of spades. When he came in later with the queen of hearts he switched to the queen of diamonds. The difference was that the defenders could now cash three diamonds and defeat the contract.

Having noted this excellent defence, let's go back to the declarer's play at trick two after he had won the first trick with the 10 of spades. Both declarers, you may remember, crossed to the king of hearts to take the club finesse. Disregarding the legend that the king of clubs is always single, do you think this was good play?

It certainly was not, because if the king of clubs is held by East, nothing he can do will embarrass the declarer. If a spade comes back South will simply finesse the jack of hearts, ensuring nine tricks.

If West happens to have the guarded king of clubs, then at least you will have lost nothing by playing the suit from your own hand. The defenders might possibly be able to take four tricks in diamonds, but they will have to do this immediately and it won't be easy if West holds something like Q 10x in the suit. If West does not attack diamonds, declarer will take the heart finesse towards the safe hand.

Interesting, is it not, that this contract of 3NT, always the touchstone of expert play, offers so many opportunities for clever handling by both sides.

14

Mountain Air

Suppose that your partner opens 1 NT, 16–18 in the system, and you have the good fortune to hold in response:

♠ K Q 7 3
♡ A Q 10
◇ A Q 6 5
♣ 7 2

You are in the small slam range, obviously. Two questions arise: will you aim to play in a suit if you can find a 4–4 fit, and if so, how will you discover a 4–4 fit in a minor suit?

When you can be sure of 33 points in the combined hands there is much to be said for going straight to 6 NT. This way, you escape the annoyance that can arise if your trump suit breaks badly. Somehow, in 6 NT a good player will usually find a way to develop his twelfth trick.

However, most players would search for the 4–4 fit. If you are playing transfer responses, then the sequence

1 NT	2 ◇
2 ♡	2 ♠

can be enlisted to initiate a Baron sequence; that is to say, opener may now rebid 2 NT with a minimum 4–3–3–3 type but will normally bid his 4–card suits upwards, while responder does the same. This way, you will never miss a 4–4 fit (unless responder chooses to close shop in 3 NT).

In a rubber bridge game at Crans-sur-Sierre the responder on the North hand below used a different method: over 1 NT he jumped to 5 NT, declaring that this exhorted South to name his lowest four-card suit. South in fact bid six clubs and the partnership ended in the natural contract of 6 NT.

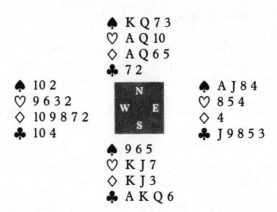

             ♠ K Q 7 3
             ♡ A Q 10
             ◇ A Q 6 5
             ♣ 7 2
♠ 10 2   ♠ A J 8 4
♡ 9 6 3 2   ♡ 8 5 4
◇ 10 9 8 7 2   ◇ 4
♣ 10 4   ♣ J 9 8 5 3
             ♠ 9 6 5
             ♡ K J 7
             ◇ K J 3
             ♣ A K Q 6

West led a diamond, won by the king, and at trick two declarer played a low spade to the queen. East, naturally, played low. South might have come back to hand for another spade lead, but instead he cashed two more diamonds, East throwing a heart and a club, followed by three rounds of hearts. By this time the position was:

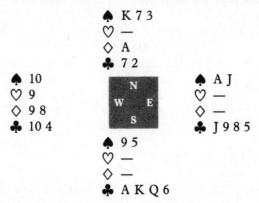

             ♠ K 7 3
             ♡ —
             ◇ A
             ♣ 7 2
♠ 10   ♠ A J
♡ 9   ♡ —
◇ 9 8   ◇ —
♣ 10 4   ♣ J 9 8 5
             ♠ 9 5
             ♡ —
             ◇ —
             ♣ A K Q 6

Since West was known to hold the thirteenth heart (East having thrown a heart early on), the declarer was committed to playing East for the ace of spades. On the diamond ace East was unhappy. When he threw a club, South discarded a spade and made four tricks in clubs.

Whether South really played the hand well is difficult to say, but two interesting points struck me.

On the first round of spades it would have been clever play for West, holding 10 2, to play the 10. This would surely have tempted the declarer to play him for J 10 or A 10, or possibly A 10 x.

Secondly, East's early discard of a small heart was a small mistake. It enabled South later on to place West with the thirteenth heart and so, indirectly, forced him to play East for the ace of spades. When discarding, try not to give the declarer the count.

15

Cover Point

This was a competitive deal, as you can see, the type that will produce many different contracts in a pairs event.

Dealer South   N–S vulnerable

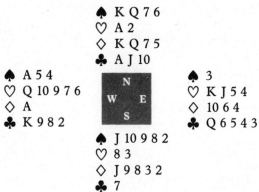

```
                ♠ K Q 7 6
                ♡ A 2
                ◇ K Q 7 5
                ♣ A J 10
♠ A 5 4                         ♠ 3
♡ Q 10 9 7 6        N           ♡ K J 5 4
◇ A             W       E       ◇ 10 6 4
♣ K 9 8 2           S           ♣ Q 6 5 4 3
                ♠ J 10 9 8 2
                ♡ 8 3
                ◇ J 9 8 3 2
                ♣ 7
```

Some East–West pairs played in four hearts and made it. The popular contract for North–South was four spades, sometimes doubled.

To my mind, this would be a sensible auction:

South	West	North	East
No	1♡	Dble	3♡
No	No	Dble	No
4♠	No	No	No

Many players, I know, would bid three spades on the first round, believing that they were being properly audacious. There is a truth

[44]

about overbids of this kind that players consistently overlook: if indeed nine tricks can be made on the North–South cards, North will almost surely be bidding four spades, which will go one down and may not be a save of any kind. When North doubles again, South can reasonably bid the game. You may say that, on this reasoning, North–South can never play in *three* spades. Well, few things are perfect in the world of competitive bidding.

This contract of four spades was reached at three tables and was doubled at two of them. Not that either defender has a sound double; but in a pairs it is reasonable to take the view that four spades undoubled, and one down, may not be a good result for East–West, but 200 will be better than average.

Look at the full deal and decide what you think should happen in four spades after the lead of the ace of diamonds, followed by a low heart. In practice, there were three different lines of play.

The first declarer, rather innocent, won the second trick with the ace of hearts and advanced the king of spades. West won, led a heart to his partner's king, and ruffed the diamond return. One down.

At the second table South was a more knowledgeable player. Recognising the danger of a diamond ruff (why otherwise would West have made the unattractive lead of the ace of diamonds?) he put into operation the Scissors Coup—or, as it used to be called, the Coup Without a Name. He cashed dummy's ace of clubs and followed with the 10, discarding his second heart. Now West could not give his partner the lead and the contract was made.

You may wonder, can anyone beat that? As declarer, no, but at the third table the defence excelled. South began on the same lines as the previous declarer—ace and 10 of clubs. 'That's an odd thing to do in four spades', East thought to himself; and it wasn't long before East inserted the *queen* of clubs, spoiling South's plan. 'I was always taught to cover an honour with an honour', he remarked modestly.

Blind Leads Are for Deaf Players

Some writers on the game set out a table of leads, stating that the correct lead from such-and-such a combination is such-and-such: the king from K Q J, fourth best from four to an honour in partner's suit, down to the despised tail—ace from A Q x, x from K J x, and the like.

This teaching is responsible for many poor defences. The most one should say is that such-and-such a lead is the conventional lead in ordinary circumstances. Observe this performance from pairs play:

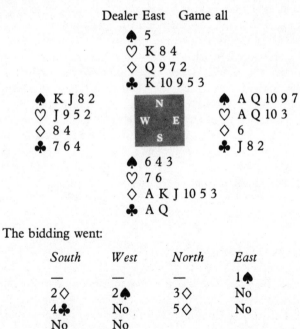

Dealer East   Game all

♠ 5
♡ K 8 4
◇ Q 9 7 2
♣ K 10 9 5 3

♠ K J 8 2   ♠ A Q 10 9 7
♡ J 9 5 2   ♡ A Q 10 3
◇ 8 4   ◇ 6
♣ 7 6 4   ♣ J 8 2

♠ 6 4 3
♡ 7 6
◇ A K J 10 5 3
♣ A Q

The bidding went:

South	West	North	East
—	—	—	1♠
2◇	2♠	3◇	No
4♣	No	5◇	No
No	No		

South's four clubs was a game invitation, but North's acceptance, with no ace in his hand, was doubtful.

West made the conventional lead of a low spade. East won and sensibly cashed the ace of hearts. This saved the overtrick and would have been very necessary if South's diamonds had been headed by A J 10 instead of A K.

'You might have tried some other lead', East suggested to his partner. 'And if a spade, surely the king is better.'

'I was always taught to lead the fourth best of my partner's suit', said West, as though that ended the matter.

But when a defender has only one possible trick and is capable of holding the lead, he should usually begin with his winner. On this occasion a switch to ♡ J, after ♠ K, would have been easy to find.

Another time for an unorthodox lead occurs when you can be fairly sure that your partner will not have enough entries to play to your strength. For example, with K 109xxx (or Q 109xxx) and two aces it may be right to lead the king (or queen) so that you will catch a singleton honour in your partner's hand. The Mexican international, George Rosenkranz, described a deal where the high card was right for a different reason:

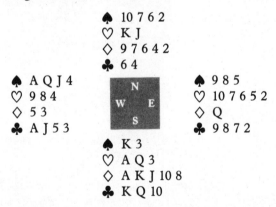

```
            ♠ 10 7 6 2
            ♡ K J
            ◇ 9 7 6 4 2
            ♣ 6 4
♠ A Q J 4              ♠ 9 8 5
♡ 9 8 4      N         ♡ 10 7 6 5 2
◇ 5 3      W   E       ◇ Q
♣ A J 5 3    S         ♣ 9 8 7 2
            ♠ K 3
            ♡ A Q 3
            ◇ A K J 10 8
            ♣ K Q 10
```

South opened 2 NT, North bid three clubs (Stayman), and when South finished in 3 NT it was apparent that he did not hold a four-card major. West, relying on his own hand, began with the *ace* of spades. East gave the count by playing low and West then followed with the 4 of spades. Holding the declarer to nine tricks produced an excellent score in a pairs game.

17

Rock That Cradle

This deal, at any rate when compared to the one preceding, may look rather ordinary, but it has its instructive side. It occurred during a world pairs event in Monte Carlo.

Dealer North   E–W vulnerable

```
              ♠ Q J 7 3
              ♡ A 8 6
              ◊ 6 5
              ♣ A K Q 9
♠ 10 9 2                        ♠ A 8 6 4
♡ Q 10 5 3                      ♡ J 9 2
◊ 10 7 4                        ◊ A J 8 2
♣ 7 3 2                         ♣ J 8
              ♠ K 5
              ♡ K 7 4
              ◊ K Q 9 3
              ♣ 10 6 5 4
```

South played in 3 NT and West began with a low heart. East's jack was allowed to hold and he returned the 9. South won this in dummy and led a low spade to the king, which held.

It is easy, as you can see, to make nine tricks on the deal, but is it easy to make ten? On the surface, you should make two spades, two hearts, two diamonds and four clubs. But there are entry problems. The moment you try to set up a second trick in spades, for example, the defence will play a third round. Evidently you must play on diamonds next, so you enter dummy with a club and lead a diamond to the queen (slightly better than the king in these situations when you want to smoke out the ace).

Suppose you have concluded by this time that East holds both the missing aces. In that case, the next card is a small surprise: it is good play to cash the king of hearts before crossing to the king of clubs. Now you are looking at:

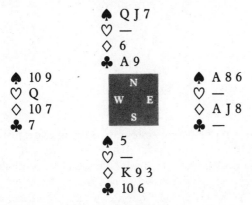

```
              ♠ Q J 7
              ♡ —
              ◇ 6
              ♣ A 9
  ♠ 10 9                      ♠ A 8 6
  ♡ Q              N          ♡ —
  ◇ 10 7      W       E       ◇ A J 8
  ♣ 7              S          ♣ —
              ♠ 5
              ♡ —
              ◇ K 9 3
              ♣ 10 6
```

You are in dummy and you lead the ace of clubs. Now if East discards a diamond you play a low club from hand and follow with the 6 of diamonds; but if East discards a spade you play the 10 of clubs under the ace and follow with the queen of spades. The play is of the same family as the see-saw squeeze, where depending on the defence you may or may not overtake the card you have led.

Note the technique on this deal. You don't play off four rounds of clubs early on, because this will destroy your own communications. You play the third round only when you have made the preliminary moves in the other suits.

18

Long View

Of all items of advice, none is so foolish as the one that instructs a player always to respond in a four-card major. Anyone who has played rubber bridge over a long period knows how profitable it is to conceal major suits such as K J 9 x or Q 10 8 x. A certain type of defender will commonly lead from x x x of an unbid major. The importance of discovering every 4–4 fit on fairly balanced hands is *greatly* exaggerated. Sometimes it is easier to make 3 NT than game in the major.

Equally foolish, in my opinion, is the tendency to respond on very weak suits when the hand is likely to be played eventually in notrumps. The following deal was an example:

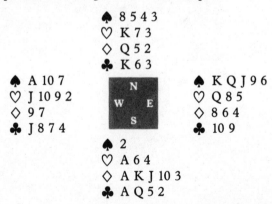

```
                    ♠ 8 5 4 3
                    ♡ K 7 3
                    ◇ Q 5 2
                    ♣ K 6 3
♠ A 10 7                              ♠ K Q J 9 6
♡ J 10 9 2          N                ♡ Q 8 5
◇ 9 7            W     E              ◇ 8 6 4
♣ J 8 7 4           S                ♣ 10 9
                    ♠ 2
                    ♡ A 6 4
                    ◇ A K J 10 3
                    ♣ A Q 5 2
```

In a team-of-four match South at one table opened one diamond and North responded one spade. The bidding then followed this undignified course:

South	North
1◇	1♠
2♣	2◇
2♡	2NT
3NT	No

East led the king of spades and the defence took the first five tricks.

At the other table North had the sense to respond 1 NT and the bidding continued:

South	North
1◇	1NT
3♣	3◇
3♡	4♣
5◇	No

This was good bidding, but the play in five diamonds is not so easy as it may look. West leads the jack of hearts and although the South hand contains more entries than the dummy it is necessary to win the first trick with the king of hearts.

The general plan is to test the clubs early on. South draws two rounds of trumps with the ace and king, then plays ace of clubs, a club to the king, and a club from dummy in this position:

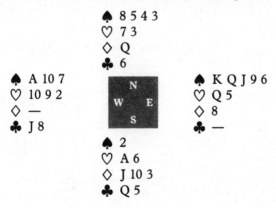

```
                ♠ 8 5 4 3
                ♡ 7 3
                ◇ Q
                ♣ 6
  ♠ A 10 7          N          ♠ K Q J 9 6
  ♡ 10 9 2      W       E      ♡ Q 5
  ◇ —                          ◇ 8
  ♣ J 8             S          ♣ —
                ♠ 2
                ♡ A 6
                ◇ J 10 3
                ♣ Q 5
```

If East does not ruff, South will simply win with the queen and ruff the club loser with dummy's queen of diamonds. Suppose that East does ruff and exits with the queen of hearts. Now, owing to his far-sighted play at trick one, South can win with the ace, discard a heart on the queen of clubs, and ruff the heart loser.

You will find that you can't do this if you win the opening heart lead in your own hand.

19

Perhaps It Was Anti-Goldschmidt

Pierre Béguin was playing in one of the big pairs events that are held in Paris when two young men came to the table and announced that they were playing 'Two Clubs with Goldschmidt'. To judge from their accents and hirsute appearance, they were students of some kind.

'If this Goldschmidt turns up, perhaps you'll explain it to us', Pierre remarked.

The first two boards were uneventful. This was the third:

Dealer South   N–S vulnerable

```
                    ♠ 8 6 4 3 2
                    ♡ 7 4 3
                    ◇ 10
                    ♣ 9 6 5 2
    ♠ A Q 9 5                      ♠ 7
    ♡ K 9 2           N            ♡ J 10 6 5
    ◇ A J 7 4     W       E        ◇ K 8 6 3 2
    ♣ J 8             S            ♣ A 7 3
                    ♠ K J 10
                    ♡ A Q 8
                    ◇ Q 9 5
                    ♣ K Q 10 4
```

South opened 1 NT and Béguin, West, made the sort of unsound double that players sometimes risk in pairs play. This was followed by three passes. You might expect North to take some action, but perhaps this would have been anti-Goldschmidt.

With no very attractive lead, West began with a low diamond to the king. He won the diamond return with the jack and was happy to see the queen fall under the ace. On the fourth and fifth diamonds South parted with a heart and the 10 of clubs.

A heart went to the queen and king and a heart was returned. South led the king of clubs, won by East, the jack of hearts was cashed, and this was the position when East played his fourth heart:

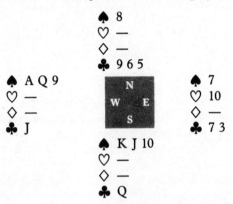

```
                    ♠ 8
                    ♡ —
                    ◇ —
                    ♣ 9 6 5
  ♠ A Q 9                          ♠ 7
  ♡ —              N               ♡ 10
  ◇ —           W     E            ◇ —
  ♣ J              S               ♣ 7 3
                    ♠ K J 10
                    ♡ —
                    ◇ —
                    ♣ Q
```

South discarded a spade and West made the last three tricks. Six down, 1700.

As the young men left the table, Pierre said he was most interested in this Goldschmidt convention: would they explain it to him after the tournament?

20

Ministry of Misinformation

There are moments in bridge when a play that would normally be most inept is exactly right. An example occurred on this deal:

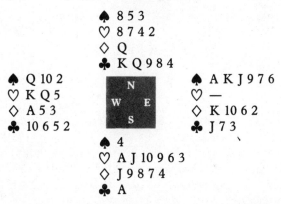

```
              ♠ 8 5 3
              ♡ 8 7 4 2
              ◇ Q
              ♣ K Q 9 8 4
♠ Q 10 2            N            ♠ A K J 9 7 6
♡ K Q 5      W          E        ♡ —
◇ A 5 3            S            ◇ K 10 6 2
♣ 10 6 5 2                       ♣ J 7 3
              ♠ 4
              ♡ A J 10 9 6 3
              ◇ J 9 8 7 4
              ♣ A
```

It was game all at rubber bridge and both sides had 60 below. Thus a keenly contested auction was to be expected.

South	West	North	East
—	No	No	1♠
2♡	2NT	3♡	3♠
4♡	Dble	No	No
No			

West led the 2 of spades to his partner's king. A strong player in East's position would realise that this was not the moment to assist the declarer to reduce his trump length; he would lead a club or a diamond at trick two. However, not many players would think of that and East in practice led a second spade. South ruffed and led a

[55]

diamond. West went up with the ace and (still more foolishly) led a third spade.

Since East would undoubtedly have led a trump at trick two if he had held one, South could be sure that West held K Q x over him. His only chance was to bring about an endplay. After a diamond ruff and a club to the ace this was the position:

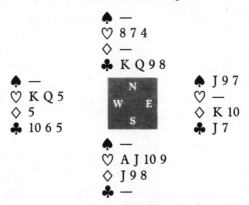

```
                    ♠ —
                    ♡ 8 7 4
                    ◇ —
                    ♣ K Q 9 8
    ♠ —                            ♠ J 9 7
    ♡ K Q 5          N             ♡ —
    ◇ 5          W       E         ◇ K 10
    ♣ 10 6 5         S             ♣ J 7
                    ♠ —
                    ♡ A J 10 9
                    ◇ J 9 8
                    ♣ —
```

South ruffed a diamond, then played three rounds of clubs, ruffing the third round. Now he was down to ♡ A J 10 and it wasn't difficult to endplay West.

As I remarked earlier, it wasn't good play by East to return a spade at trick two or by West to lead a third round when in with the ace of diamonds. But despite these mistakes the defenders had one further chance.

Look again at the second diagram. At the point when South ruffed the third round of diamonds East should have played the *king*. This could hardly cost and would surely have induced South to misread the distribution. Placing West with the fourth diamond and two clubs, he would have played the king of clubs and ruffed a club, then led his last diamond, expecting West to follow suit. But West would have been able to ruff and exit with his last club.

So the lesson is: when you know that the cards you play cannot matter, don't miss a chance to misinform declarer about the distribution.

21

Long Sight

The problem described below has appeared from time to time in various publications, and the reason I include it now is that a new solution has been proposed. The original play has usually been ascribed to one of the Italian champions, but one is bound to have doubts about that because it is the unamiable practice of Italian journalists to attribute any invented, or sensational, play to a named player.

♠ K 10 3
♥ 8 7 6
♦ K Q 10 4 2
♣ K 7

♠ A 8 4
♥ 2
♦ 9 8 7
♣ Q 10 8 5 4 3

South plays in four spades after this sequence:

South	West	North	East
1♠	No	2♦	2♥
No	No	3♠	No
4♠	No	No	No

Sitting West, you lead your singleton heart. Your partner wins and returns the queen of hearts. South covers with the king and you ruff with ♠4. What is your next move?

Well, your next move should be to the dog-house, because you have abandoned all chance of beating the contract. The full hand is:

[57]

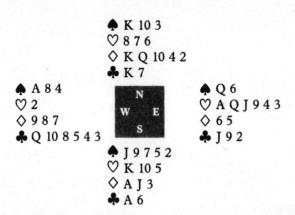

```
                    ♠ K 10 3
                    ♡ 8 7 6
                    ◇ K Q 10 4 2
                    ♣ K 7
   ♠ A 8 4            N              ♠ Q 6
   ♡ 2                              ♡ A Q J 9 4 3
   ◇ 9 8 7        W       E         ◇ 6 5
   ♣ Q 10 8 5 4 3      S            ♣ J 9 2
                    ♠ J 9 7 5 2
                    ♡ K 10 5
                    ◇ A J 3
                    ♣ A 6
```

If you ruff with the 4 of spades and exit with a diamond or a club, South can hardly go wrong in the trump suit. Knowing that East has a good heart to cash, he will have no choice but to play West for A x of spades (after the ruff) or A x x. East will never come in to cash the jack of hearts.

The traditional account of the play is that West ruffed with the *ace* of spades and so established an entry for his partner's queen. But there is another quite valid solution: West does not ruff at all—he simply discards a diamond or a club. Then again, East's queen of trumps becomes an entry card.

Note, also, that if West held A x in spades it would be essential to ruff with the ace because partner might hold a doubleton Q x. One day—who knows—you might ruff with the ace from A x to construct an entry for partner's singleton king.

22

Open Choice

In a pairs tournament would you like to play this hand in seven clubs, seven spades, or 7NT?

Dealer North   Game all

                    ♠ K 8 7 5
                    ♡ A K 6
                    ♢ A K 6 5
                    ♣ K J

♠ Q 2   ♠ J 9 3
♡ J 10 8 7 4 3   ♡ Q 9
♢ J 8 2   ♢ Q 10 9 7 3
♣ 10 7   ♣ 9 3 2

                    ♠ A 10 6 4
                    ♡ 5 2
                    ♢ 4
                    ♣ A Q 8 6 5 4

Seven clubs can be made if you follow a particular line: draw trumps, ruff the third diamond, and squeeze East at the finish in spades and diamonds. You might fail in practice because there are other squeeze possibilities.

Seven spades is obviously impossible. On some hands it is possible to pick up an enemy trump holding of Qx opposite Jxx, but not here, because you cannot run off the club suit in preparation for the trump coup.

In one of the Philip Morris pairs events in Europe, John Collings found himself in 7NT after this sequence:

South	West	North	East
—	—	1♣(1)	1◇(2)
1NT(3)	2♡	2NT	No
3♣	No	3♠ (4)	No
4NT	No	6♣(5)	No
7NT	No	No	No

(1) Conventional, 16 points upwards.
(2) Some players like to intervene after a strong opening bid. It is worse than pointless when you are not even depriving the opponents of bidding space.
(3) Conventional, denoting the number of controls.
(4) Conventional, showing the quality of the top cards in clubs.
(5) Expressing the total of controls.

There might be an argument about some of these notes, but they express the general idea.

Against a heart, club or spade lead the contract is not difficult to play, thanks mainly to the fatuous bids made by the opposition. Placing West with the long hearts, South cashes ace and king of hearts, then runs off the winners in the black suits. There is a double squeeze at the finish, West needing to keep a heart and East a spade, with diamonds as the pivot suit.

West struck a diamond lead, but Collings played for this ending:

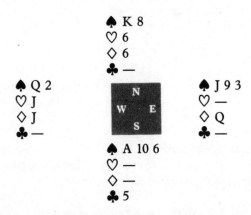

If West, on the last club, parts with the jack of diamonds his partner will be squeezed. His best try is a low spade, but then partner's spades can be picked up. This is a guard squeeze, the special feature being that West has to expose his partner to the spade finesse.

23

First Cousin

After the deal below had been played in a pairs event, one of the players was button-holing everyone in sight, asking 'What did you do on board so-and-so?' It was clear that he wanted to relate his own performance.

Dealer South   Love all

♠ 3
♡ A Q 6
◇ J 7 6 5 4
♣ K 6 4 3

♠ 7 6 4 2   ♠ Q 10 9 5
♡ K J 8 5   ♡ 10 4 3 2
◇ 8   ◇ K 9 3
♣ A 7 5 2   ♣ Q 8

♠ A K J 8
♡ 9 7
◇ A Q 10 2
♣ J 10 9

South had opened 1 NT, a call that I find repulsive, and had been raised to 3 NT. West had led the 5 of hearts.

Safety plays are by no means always advisable in pairs play, of course, but even so I would have been inclined to play low from dummy rather than finesse the queen, which would surely be bad if East held the king. But our hero, or anti-hero, won with the queen and led the jack of diamonds, unblocking the 10 when East played low. After five rounds of diamonds, on which West had discarded two spades, South judged it safe finesse the jack of spades. The ace of spades was cashed, leaving:

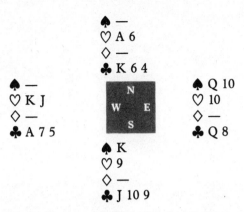

```
              ♠ —
              ♡ A 6
              ◇ —
              ♣ K 6 4
♠ —                          ♠ Q 10
♡ K J          N             ♡ 10
◇ —         W     E          ◇ —
♣ A 7 5        S             ♣ Q 8
              ♠ K
              ♡ 9
              ◇ —
              ♣ J 10 9
```

'I had the cards pretty well placed', South went on. 'I cashed the
king of spades, West discarding a club and dummy a heart. Then I
played a club to the king, returned a club, and made twelve tricks.
An unusual sort of squeeze, wasn't it? It gave us a clear top.'

When he told me this story, I remembered another deal of the
same kind (no. 21). 'I don't see it', I said.

'What do your mean, you don't see it? Do you want me to write
down all the cards?'

'No. What do you say West threw on the king of spades?'

At last the penny dropped. If West discards the ace of clubs in
the endgame, creating an entry for his partner, the defenders make a
club and a spade. The play is a first cousin to the Deschapelles
Coup, where (in the strict form) a defender leads a high card to
create an entry for his partner.

24

Green Light

North opens 1 NT on the deal below and South, not playing any form of transfer, bids two hearts, which is passed out. One reason why North–South are not playing transfer responses is that this deal was described nearly 25 years ago, before such methods were common.

Dealer North   Game all

♠ J 6 4
♥ K 5 2
♦ A J 7
♣ A K 6 3

♠ A K Q 2
♥ 3
♦ 10 8 4
♣ 9 8 7 5 4

♠ 10 7 5
♥ A Q 9 7
♦ K 9 3
♣ J 10 2

♠ 9 8 3
♥ J 10 8 6 4
♦ Q 6 5 2
♣ Q

Defending against two hearts, West cashes three top spades, then leads a diamond. East wins with the king and returns a club, taken by South's queen. This leaves:

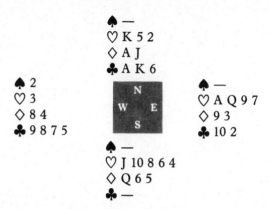

```
              ♠ —
              ♡ K 5 2
              ◇ A J
              ♣ A K 6
♠ 2                              ♠ —
♡ 3          ┌─────────┐         ♡ A Q 9 7
◇ 8 4        │   N     │         ◇ 9 3
♣ 9 8 7 5    │ W     E │         ♣ 10 2
             │   S     │
             └─────────┘
              ♠ —
              ♡ J 10 8 6 4
              ◇ Q 6 5
              ♣ —
```

South has lost four tricks and it looks as though he will be one down. Yet, according to the story, he finished *two* down. How can he possibly do that? He is going to run the jack of hearts, losing to the queen; the next heart will go to the king and ace, and a simple finesse will pick up East's 9 and 7 of trumps.

You might look at this for a long while without attaching your mind to the answer. The point is that when South runs the jack of hearts East wins, not with the queen, but with the ace. The effect of this is that when South is next in he may lead the 10 of hearts in the hope of pinning East's 9. This is a way—the only way—to lose three trump tricks.

I'm not sure I believe the story—in fact, I'm sure I don't—but it is an interesting thought and there must be other situations of the same kind. Similar plays with K J, Q 10 or J 9 are familiar. For example:

```
              Q 10 7 4
    A J 9                 5 3 2
              K 8 6
```

When South leads the 6 the jack from West may have a surprising effect.

25

No Learned Comments

I'm not quite sure what to say about this deal. It looks a tricky affair in six clubs. Most tournament players, after a trump lead, would go into hibernation for several minutes; but at rubber bridge a player not generally held in great esteem rattled off cards in quick succession and claimed the contract five tricks from the finish.

Dealer North   Game all

♠ A 8 6 3
♥ A Q 9 3 2
♦ —
♣ A K 8 3

♠ Q 7 2
♥ K 10 8 4
♦ 10 5 2
♣ J 10 9

♠ 10 5 4
♥ J 7 5
♦ K 9 8 6 3
♣ 4 2

♠ K J 9
♥ 6
♦ A Q J 7 4
♣ Q 7 6 5

This was the bidding:

South	North
—	1♡
2◇	2♠
3♣(1)	4♣
4♠	6♣(2)
No	

[66]

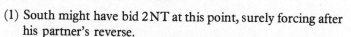

(1) South might have bid 2NT at this point, surely forcing after his partner's reverse.

(2) Thinking, presumably, that if South's three clubs had not been a genuine suit he would revert to six spades.

Maybe it was as well that South played the contract and not his partner. He won the club lead with the queen, played a heart to dummy's ace—no finesse, you notice—and ruffed a heart; then a club to the king and another heart ruff. A low diamond was ruffed, the last trump was drawn, and the position was then:

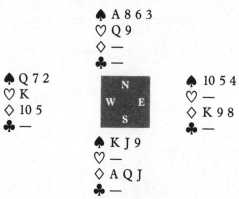

The declarer led a heart from dummy, and when East showed out he discarded a diamond and claimed the contract. West, at this point, had to lead into either the spade or diamond tenace. Was it really so easy?

26

Sensibly Silent

When you're dead, lie down, might be the theme of this deal, which was described in the Norwegian magazine. It is a striking example of playing the card you are known to hold—or will shortly be known to hold.

Dealer South   Game all

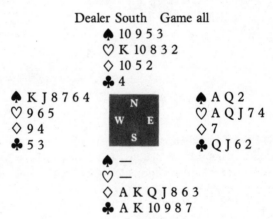

♠ 10 9 5 3
♡ K 10 8 3 2
◇ 10 5 2
♣ 4

♠ K J 8 7 6 4
♡ 9 6 5
◇ 9 4
♣ 5 3

♠ A Q 2
♡ A Q J 7 4
◇ 7
♣ Q J 6 2

♠ —
♡ —
◇ A K Q J 8 6 3
♣ A K 10 9 8 7

South opens with a conventional two clubs and the bidding continues:

South	West	North	East
2♣	No	2♡(1)	No(2)
3◇	No	3♡	No
4♣	No	5◇(3)	No
7◇	No	No	No(4)

(1) It is a modern fashion to play two hearts as the negative, two diamonds as a semi-positive. Don't ask me why.

[68]

(2) Most tournament players would sweep in with a double of the artificial bid.

(3) Fairly bold on his moderate values, but a good bid, surely.

(4) Still sensibly silent. It is obvious that South is void in both majors.

South ruffed the spade lead and led the ace of clubs. It is apparent that the slam is lay-down, since declarer can ruff one club with $\Diamond 2$ and one with $\Diamond 10$, establishing the suit. What can go wrong?

A simple thing. Knowing that his queen of clubs was a dead duck, East played it on the first round. Consider this from South's angle. Thinking that the club queen might be a singleton, he drew two rounds of trumps before laying down the king of clubs. If West had held the length in clubs this would have been safe; as it was, he could ruff only once and was left with a club loser.

There the story ended. It was clever play by East, certainly, but should South have fallen into the trap? Suppose the club situation had been:

4

6 5 3   Q J 2

A K 10 9 8 7

Now many players in East's position might drop the queen of clubs under the ace on the first round of the suit. They might even make the same play from Qx. This means that after cashing two high diamonds and following with king and 10 of clubs, South is going to have a guess whether to ruff the third club or let it run. It may be better play to draw one round of trumps, then ruff a club with $\Diamond 5$. This will be fatal only if East began with a singleton queen of clubs and is able to overruff.

Tricky Trump Trick

In the early days much used to be written about 'prepared bids'. Nowadays the phrase is seldom heard. South, on this deal from a pairs event, was old-fashioned enough to open one spade so that he would be able to show the second suit without reversing. There is a hazard in this procedure, as the bidding showed.

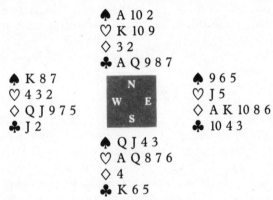

♠ A 10 2
♡ K 10 9
◇ 3 2
♣ A Q 9 8 7

♠ K 8 7　　　　　　　　　　　♠ 9 6 5
♡ 4 3 2　　　　　　　　　　　♡ J 5
◇ Q J 9 7 5　　　　　　　　　◇ A K 10 8 6
♣ J 2　　　　　　　　　　　　♣ 10 4 3

♠ Q J 4 3
♡ A Q 8 7 6
◇ 4
♣ K 6 5

South opened one spade and this was the continuation:

South	North
1♠	2♣
2♡	3◇
3♡	4♠
No	

North, having already bid the fourth-suit three diamonds, should have bid simply three spades over three hearts, but whether the partnership would have finished in hearts is uncertain.

As can easily be seen, twelve tricks can be made in any of three suits, but when Jean Besse and Tony Trad were East–West the result in four spades was less satisfactory for the declarer.

Confident that he could manage a 4–2 trump break, South ruffed the second diamond, led the queen of spades and followed with a second spade to the 10. Now, to allow for a possible 4–2 division, he played off winners in clubs. Instead of ruffing the third round Besse discarded a diamond, and on the fourth club East threw a heart and West another diamond. This left:

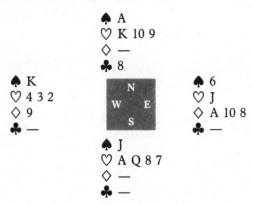

♠ A
♡ K 10 9
◇ —
♣ 8

♠ K
♡ 4 3 2
◇ 9
♣ —

♠ 6
♡ J
◇ A 10 8
♣ —

♠ J
♡ A Q 8 7
◇ —
♣ —

On dummy's fifth club East discarded his second heart and the defence made two more tricks. It was a very poor result for North–South.

There are many variations of this type of defence. Picture the following deal:

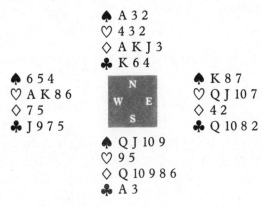

♠ A 3 2
♡ 4 3 2
◇ A K J 3
♣ K 6 4

♠ 6 5 4
♡ A K 8 6
◇ 7 5
♣ J 9 7 5

♠ K 8 7
♡ Q J 10 7
◇ 4 2
♣ Q 10 8 2

♠ Q J 10 9
♡ 9 5
◇ Q 10 9 8 6
♣ A 3

Playing in four spades (the only possible game contract, as it happens), South ruffs the third round of hearts and plays the queen of spades, followed by the jack, which holds! To allow for a 4–2 trump break, declarer plays on diamonds. On the third round East discards his remaining heart, West ruffs, and a heart lead promotes the king of trumps.

28

Not an Optimist

The play of the cards, in one sense, is just a chain of deductions.
Bernasconi did not jump over any of the links in the chain when he
played this deal during a match between teams from Zurich and
Geneva.

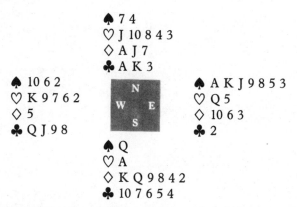

```
              ♠ 7 4
              ♡ J 10 8 4 3
              ◇ A J 7
              ♣ A K 3
♠ 10 6 2                        ♠ A K J 9 8 5 3
♡ K 9 7 6 2      N              ♡ Q 5
◇ 5           W     E           ◇ 10 6 3
♣ Q J 9 8         S            ♣ 2
              ♠ Q
              ♡ A
              ◇ K Q 9 8 4 2
              ♣ 10 7 6 5 4
```

East-West were vulnerable and Pietro was South. This was the
bidding:

South	West	North	East
—	—	1♡	3♠
4◇	4♠	No	No
5♣	No	5◇	No
No	No		

West led a spade to the king and East played a second round,
ruffed by the declarer.

The contract would be easy if the diamonds were 2–2 (permitting South to ruff the fourth round of clubs if necessary), or if the clubs broke well. But Pietro, like most good players, is not an optimist when playing the cards. Also, East's three spade overcall was not a favourable sign.

South began with a little exploration. After ruffing the second spade he cashed the ace of hearts, crossed to the ace of diamonds, and ruffed a low heart. When East's queen appeared on the second round it seemed likely that the hearts would be breaking 5–2. East would not have made the pre-emptive overcall with strong spades and K Q x over the opener's suit.

On the king of diamonds West, after a little thought, discarded his third spade. (It might be a mistake to throw a heart, enabling the declarer to run dummy's jack of hearts and establish two winners.) The end position was fairly clear:

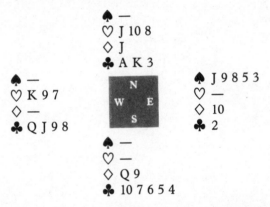

```
                    ♠ —
                    ♡ J 10 8
                    ◇ J
                    ♣ A K 3
     ♠ —                              ♠ J 9 8 5 3
     ♡ K 9 7          N               ♡ —
     ◇ —           W     E            ◇ 10
     ♣ Q J 9 8         S              ♣ 2
                    ♠ —
                    ♡ —
                    ◇ Q 9
                    ♣ 10 7 6 5 4
```

When the declarer led a low diamond towards the jack, West was reluctant to part with any of his jewels. Either a heart or a club would enable South to establish an extra trick. Bernasconi showed his cards and West surrendered.

29

Accurate Assessment

On this deal from rubber bridge the players holding the North–South cards reached a small slam with a combined count of 23 and played well to make it, especially as the trumps did not break well.

> ♠ K 3
> ♡ A K Q 7 5
> ◇ A 6 3
> ♣ 8 5 2

◇ 8 led

> ♠ A Q 10 8 7 6
> ♡ 8 2
> ◇ J 10 9 5 2
> ♣ —

North–South were vulnerable and East was the dealer. The bidding went:

South	West	North	East
—	—	—	No
No	No	1♡	No
2♠(1)	No	3♠(2)	No
4♣	No	4◇	No
6♠(3)	No	No	No

(1) He hardly has enough for this jump response, but it turned out well.

(2) A jump response by a passed player normally shows either a

strong suit or strong support for the opener's suit. North's three spades was an intelligent choice, I think.

(3) Sporting, but they were going to get there anyway, as the North hand was quite strong.

West led the 8 of diamonds, not a happy sight for the declarer. It might be a singleton, in which case the best play might be to go up with the ace and play for a friendly division in both spades and hearts. However, this was against the odds and there were two further considerations: West was a tricky sort of player who might have underled an honour, and even if East held ◇ K̄ Q x x it was not certain that he would return a diamond at trick two, as there was no reason to place the declarer with length. After a cool assessment South played low from dummy. The king won and East then laid down the ace of clubs.

The second round of trumps brought bad news, for the full hand was:

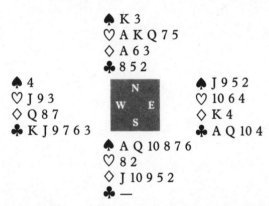

```
                    ♠ K 3
                    ♡ A K Q 7 5
                    ◇ A 6 3
                    ♣ 8 5 2
   ♠ 4                                 ♠ J 9 5 2
   ♡ J 9 3              N              ♡ 10 6 4
   ◇ Q 8 7         W        E          ◇ K 4
   ♣ K J 9 7 6 3          S            ♣ A Q 10 4
                    ♠ A Q 10 8 7 6
                    ♡ 8 2
                    ◇ J 10 9 5 2
                    ♣ —
```

The only chance now was to gauge the diamonds correctly and to find the hearts 3–3. South reflected that East probably had A Q or A K of clubs (since his partner had not led the suit, as he might have done with K Q) and that with ◇ K Q he might have opened the bidding. So he ran the jack of diamonds successfully, ruffed another club, and reached this ending:

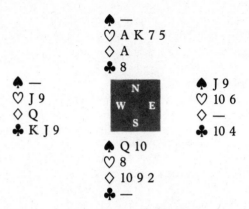

```
                    ♠ —
                    ♡ A K 7 5
                    ◇ A
                    ♣ 8
♠ —                 ┌─────────┐        ♠ J 9
♡ J 9               │    N    │        ♡ 10 6
◇ Q                 │  W   E  │        ◇ —
♣ K J 9             │    S    │        ♣ 10 4
                    └─────────┘
                    ♠ Q 10
                    ♡ 8
                    ◇ 10 9 2
                    ♣ —
```

Now three rounds of hearts ended East's chances. He ruffed the third round, but South was able to overruff, draw the last trump, and return to dummy, making the ace of diamonds and the last heart.

30

Vain Search

Some hands end in a very unexpected way. Looking at the North–South cards below, it would be difficult to foresee the ending that occurred at the table.

```
                    ♠ Q
                    ♡ A 9 6 4
                    ♢ A K Q
                    ♣ A K 10 9 2
    ♣ 6 led
                    ♠ A 10 8 3
                    ♡ K J 10 8
                    ♢ J 5
                    ♣ 8 5 3
```

The North hand is awkward for Acol players, in the sense that it is strong for one club and not ideal for two clubs. North chose one club in third position and the bidding continued:

South	North
No	1♣
1♡	3♢
3NT	4♡
4♠	6♡
No	

South's four spades was borderline, because his club holding seemed unfavourable for a slam.

On the lead of the 6 of clubs the ace was played from dummy and the 7 by East. There were several ways to play the hand. Declarer might play a ruffing game, not leading any trumps early on. Or he might try to find the queen of hearts, with chances even if the finesse failed. His actual line was to cash ace and king of hearts. The trumps broke 3–2 but the queen did not fall, as this was the full deal:

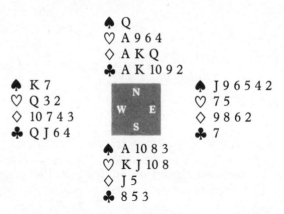

After ace and king of hearts South played a second club from hand, half expecting West to show out. But West followed with the 4, the king won, and East discarded a spade. Now the declarer cashed three top diamonds, discarding his third club, took a spade ruff, then a club ruff. This was the end position:

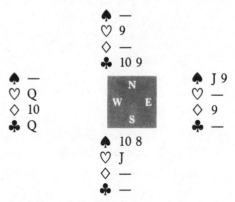

South led the 8 of spades and West, who had been looking smug since the success of his ruse in the club suit, was unable to find a good discard. When he threw a diamond, South ruffed the spade and made his twelfth trick with a club ruff. The declarer, quite a guileless player in the ordinary way, did not plan this ending, he just stumbled on it.

31

Force of Habit

Few kinds of play are more difficult then those that run contrary to all instinct and training. That pontifical remark is confirmed by the following deal from the match between Britain and Austria in the European Championship at Salsomaggiore, in Italy.

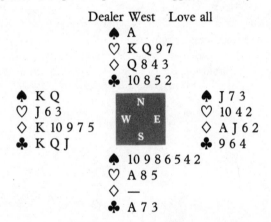

Dealer West   Love all

```
                    ♠ A
                    ♡ K Q 9 7
                    ◇ Q 8 4 3
                    ♣ 10 8 5 2
  ♠ K Q                           ♠ J 7 3
  ♡ J 6 3            N            ♡ 10 4 2
  ◇ K 10 9 7 5    W     E         ◇ A J 6 2
  ♣ K Q J            S            ♣ 9 6 4
                    ♠ 10 9 8 6 5 4 2
                    ♡ A 8 5
                    ◇ —
                    ♣ A 7 3
```

Although neither North nor South has the conventional values for an opening bid, one pair reached four spades after this sequence:

South	West	North	East
—	1◇	No	2◇
2♠	No	2NT	No
3♠	No	4♠	No
No	No		

North could read his partner for short diamonds, so it was not unreasonable to try for game.

West led the king of clubs and East played the 4. From force of habit South held up the ace, won the second round and played a spade to the ace. After three rounds of hearts the position was:

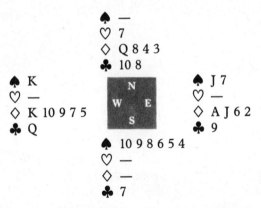

```
              ♠ —
              ♡ 7
              ◇ Q 8 4 3
              ♣ 10 8
♠ K                          ♠ J 7
♡ —           N              ♡ —
◇ K 10 9 7 5  W   E          ◇ A J 6 2
♣ Q               S          ♣ 9
              ♠ 10 9 8 6 5 4
              ♡ —
              ◇ —
              ♣ 7
```

On the thirteenth heart East ruffed low—good play—and South discarded his losing club. No good, because West also discarded a club and the defenders made their remaining trumps separately.

You see the point of the deal? If South, taking note of East's 4 of clubs on the first trick, judges the clubs to be 3–3 and considers the possibility of finding one opponent with a doubleton honour in trumps, he must depart from normal practice and capture the first club. Then the endgame is:

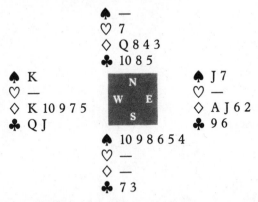

```
              ♠ —
              ♡ 7
              ◇ Q 8 4 3
              ♣ 10 8 5
♠ K                          ♠ J 7
♡ —           N              ♡ —
◇ K 10 9 7 5  W   E          ◇ A J 6 2
♣ Q J             S          ♣ 9 6
              ♠ 10 9 8 6 5 4
              ♡ —
              ◇ —
              ♣ 7 3
```

As before, South leads the 7 of hearts from dummy and discards a club. The difference is that after East has ruffed low the defenders cannot make their remaining trumps separately.

32

Two Up, Two Down

It shouldn't be too difficult to reach a grand slam on the deal below, but in a pairs event only four pairs managed it. Just as well, perhaps, for only two of them made thirteen tricks.

Deal South   Game all

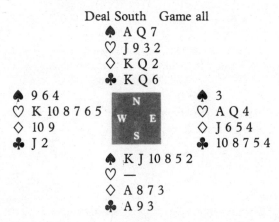

```
                    ♠ A Q 7
                    ♡ J 9 3 2
                    ◇ K Q 2
                    ♣ K Q 6
    ♠ 9 6 4                         ♠ 3
    ♡ K 10 8 7 6 5                  ♡ A Q 4
    ◇ 10 9                          ◇ J 6 5 4
    ♣ J 2                           ♣ 10 8 7 5 4
                    ♠ K J 10 8 5 2
                    ♡ —
                    ◇ A 8 7 3
                    ♣ A 9 3
```

It is the sort of hand on which you would find a different bidding sequence at almost every table. Assuming that North, in the modern fashion, is not going to force, this is a possible auction:

South	North
1♠	2♣
2◇	2♡
2♠	4♠ (1)
5♣ (2)	5◇
5♡	7♠ (3)
No	

(1) The jump to game, following a bid of the fourth suit, means that he has visions of a slam.

(2) Obviously an important control. Spare us the 'only 12 points, partner'.

(3) Well, he has plenty in hand.

West will probably begin with a trump. Since two of the four declarers in a grand slam made the contract and two did not, let's consider how they might have played the hand.

Table 1: The Innocent

How he reached seven is a small mystery, but this is how he might have played it:

Draw trumps, as instructed in early lessons. Cash six spades and three clubs. Follow with king, queen and a third diamond. (Hateful opponents have not parted with a diamond.) Play for the break, why not? One down, bad luck.

Table 2: The Keen Student

He plays in the same way until he faces the critical decision on the third round of diamonds. Isn't there something called 'The Principle of Restricted Choice', he asks himself, meaning that if West had begun with J 10 9 of diamonds he might have played his cards in a different order. Oh well, blame the experts if it goes wrong, I'm going to finesse the 8. It holds, I've made it!

Table 3: The Unlucky Expert

Ah, there's a safety play here. Draw two trumps, then play king, queen and another diamond. If they're breaking 4–2, perhaps the man with the doubleton diamond won't hold the missing trump. No good, he ruffs the third round. Typical of my luck.

Table 4: The Technician

He wins the first trick with the 7 of spades and sets about a reverse dummy. Ruff a heart at trick two, return to the queen of spades. Finding the trumps 3–1, ruff a heart, cross to the queen of diamonds; ruff a heart, cross to the queen of clubs; ruff a heart, cross to the king of clubs and draw the outstanding trump. Almost a lay-down—only a very bad distribution in one of the minor suits would have beaten it. What happened to the Unlucky Expert? He didn't make it? Oh well . . .

33

Idiots Delight

In every group of rubber bridge players there are one or two who play the cards well but consistently overbid. It is annoying, on occasions, to be on the wrong side of such adventurers.

Dealer South   Game all

```
              ♠ 8 7 5 4 3
              ♡ A 10 5
              ◇ Q 6 5
              ♣ A 6
♠ Q J 10 2                      ♠ K 9 6
♡ K 9 8 4                       ♡ J
◇ K 7                           ◇ J 10 8 4 3 2
♣ 10 4 3                        ♣ J 9 5
              ♠ A
              ♡ Q 7 6 3 2
              ◇ A 9
              ♣ K Q 8 7 2
```

West, a strong player, was playing against a hated rival in the South chair. South, it appears, opened one heart and the bidding continued:

South	North
1♡	1♠
2♣	3♡
4NT(?)	5♡
6♡	No

'I led the queen of spades', West informed me. 'Declarer won with the ace and led the queen of hearts. Would it have occurred to you to cover?'

'Probably not'.

'I didn't. A low heart to the 10 came next, then spade ruff, club to ace, spade ruff, two more clubs. You see the position now?'

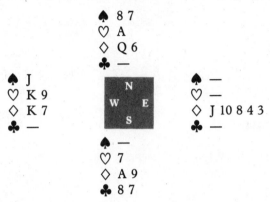

```
                    ♠ 8 7
                    ♡ A
                    ◇ Q 6
                    ♣ —
    ♠ J                          ♠ —
    ♡ K 9          N             ♡ —
    ◇ K 7      W       E         ◇ J 10 8 4 3
    ♣ —            S             ♣ —
                    ♠ —
                    ♡ 7
                    ◇ A 9
                    ♣ 8 7
```

West had to ruff the next club, dummy overruffed, and South ruffed a spade with his last heart. Then came the fifth club and West was endplayed.

'That was very pretty', I said. 'You must give him credit. The queen of hearts was a good shot. I suppose he was playing for you to hold Kxx and not cover. That's enough if the clubs are breaking 3–3.'

'There's more to it', West went on morosely. 'South said he couldn't understand why I hadn't covered the queen of hearts with the king, etc. I thought this was right at the time, but now I'm not so sure. After queen, king, ace of hearts, South ruffs a spade and leads a trump, on which I split my 9 8. Then spade ruff, club to ace, spade ruff and two more clubs, which leaves:

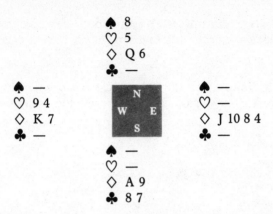

```
              ♠ 8
              ♥ 5
              ♦ Q 6
              ♣ —
♠ —                         ♠ —
♥ 9 4          N            ♥ —
♦ K 7        W   E          ♦ J 10 8 4
♣ —            S            ♣ —
              ♠ —
              ♥ —
              ♦ A 9
              ♣ 8 7
```

'South leads a club and there's no defence. Funny hand.'

34

King's Gambit

What does a military man do when he sees that his opponents match his forces at every point of the line? He moves troops from here to there, seeking to disconcert the enemy. That is the theme of the following deal:

Dealer East   N–S vulnerable

```
              ♠ A K 9 7 5 2
              ♡ K 6 5
              ◇ K
              ♣ 7 6 5
♣ 3 led
              ♠ 6 3
              ♡ A Q 8 7 3
              ◇ A Q 8 6 4 2
              ♣ —
```

South plays in an adventurous six hearts after this sequence:

South	West	North	East
—	—	—	1♣
1♡	2♣	2♠	No
3◇	No	4♡	No
6♡	No	No	No

Was North's two spades forcing? Was South justified in leaping to six hearts? Let's leave that and consider the play after West has led a low club to the ace and South has ruffed.

It's no use hoping for the red suits to divide evenly. East has opened with very few high cards and West has raised on very little, so he must have a singleton somewhere. Come to think of it, East needs to hold something like QJxx in spades, alongside his club suit, to open the bidding. So the hand begins to take shape. It must be something like this.

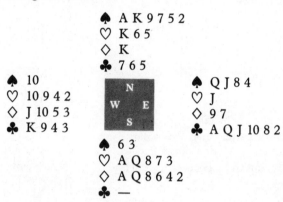

```
              ♠ A K 9 7 5 2
              ♡ K 6 5
              ◇ K
              ♣ 7 6 5
  ♠ 10                          ♠ Q J 8 4
  ♡ 10 9 4 2         N          ♡ J
  ◇ J 10 5 3      W     E       ◇ 9 7
  ♣ K 9 4 3          S          ♣ A Q J 10 8 2
              ♠ 6 3
              ♡ A Q 8 7 3
              ◇ A Q 8 6 4 2
              ♣ —
```

You have ruffed the club lead. What next? If you lead a diamond to the king, then play on trumps, hoping that at least one of the red suits will break 3–2, the hand will collapse. You may aim to ruff a low diamond to establish the suit, but then the 4–1 break in trumps will be fatal because of the lack of entries to hand.

Now try the sort of manoeuvre described above. After ruffing the club lead and crossing to the king of diamonds, play ace and king of spades!

If West ruffs and plays a club, South can accept the force, ruff a low diamond and make the rest. West's best defence is to discard a club. But this doesn't win either. Don't cash the king of hearts; instead ruff a club, cash ace of hearts, then A Q of diamonds. This leaves:

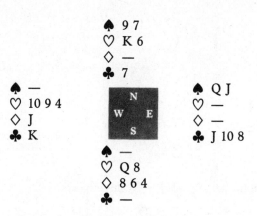

```
              ♠ 9 7
              ♡ K 6
              ◇ —
              ♣ 7
♠ —                        ♠ Q J
♡ 10 9 4      N            ♡ —
◇ J         W   E          ◇ —
♣ K           S            ♣ J 10 8
              ♠ —
              ♡ Q 8
              ◇ 8 6 4
              ♣ —
```

Now diamond ruff, club ruff, king and queen of trumps separately, and you have won the war.

35

Low Ball

You are South, playing 3 NT with these hands:

```
        ♠ K Q
        ♡ 9 5 3
        ◇ 10 9 7 4 2
        ♣ J 9 4
♠ 2 led
        ♠ A J 9 4
        ♡ A 8 6 4
        ◇ A 6
        ♣ A K 2
```

The queen of spades wins the first trick and you judge that your best chance of developing a ninth trick is to find a 3–3 break in hearts. You lead a low heart from dummy and East plays the queen. You duck this trick and West follows with the 2. This is good news, in that it is at least consistent with the possibility of an even break. Now, rather surprisingly, East advances the 5 of diamonds. What do you make of that?

The situation arose in a European Championship match between Switzerland and Italy, in the days when the Italians were on top of the world. The Swiss team was Bernasconi, Besse, Ortiz-Patino, Trad, and Vu Min, hailing respectively from Italy, Switzerland, Bolivia, Egypt, and (I imagine) Vietnam.

The declarer, Belladonna, decided that the diamond situation might be something like this:

```
            10 9 7 4 2
Q 3                        K J 8 5
            A 6
```

In this case, assuming that East had a second entry in hearts, it would be best to block the run of the high diamonds by going up with the ace. Giorgio did this, but for once he had been deceived, for the full hand was:

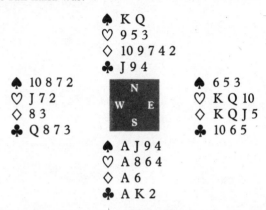

```
                    ♠ K Q
                    ♡ 9 5 3
                    ◇ 10 9 7 4 2
                    ♣ J 9 4
     ♠ 10 8 7 2        N        ♠ 6 5 3
     ♡ J 7 2                    ♡ K Q 10
     ◇ 8 3      W         E     ◇ K Q J 5
     ♣ Q 8 7 3        S        ♣ 10 6 5
                    ♠ A J 9 4
                    ♡ A 8 6 4
                    ◇ A 6
                    ♣ A K 2
```

After playing the ace of diamonds, declarer had no way to avoid going one down. It was very neat play by Bernasconi (East). I don't suppose he needed to work out the position in detail, but it would have been easy enough to estimate the declarer's likely hand. He had indicated the values for a 2 NT opening. The play so far appeared to mark him with four spades and four hearts and, since East could see nine diamonds, the odds were that South would hold two diamonds and three clubs. Looking at it another way, if South had been 3–2 in the minor suits West would have held five clubs and would have led this suit.

36

Were the Critics Right?

This was a famous deal from the 1977 world championship, played in Manila. In those days the United States fielded two teams and they met in the final.

Dealer North   Love all

In the closed room Soloway-Swanson, playing for the team described as the Challengers, played safely in 6NT. The only question here is whether, aiming to make five tricks in clubs, you should finesse or begin with ace and king. If the clubs are 4–2 it won't matter. If they are 5–1 the finesse won't help, so you may as well play for a singleton queen in the West hand. The declarer played off the top clubs and made thirteen tricks.

At the other table the Holders bid as follows:

South	North
Passell	*Hamilton*
—	1♠
3♣	3♠
4NT	5♠
5NT	6♦
7NT	No

I don't know the precise meaning of these exchanges, but it certainly seems as though South failed to discover whether his partner held the vital card, the queen of clubs.

A heart was led and South lost the contract because at one point he finessed the jack of clubs. The commentators were swift to point out that if declarer cashes nine tricks in spades, hearts and diamonds he reaches an end position where East is known to hold four clubs and West two. It becomes advisable then to play off ace and king, the only chance for four tricks in the suit.

But this analysis is superficial. Suppose that South, after the heart lead, plays three rounds of hearts and three rounds of diamonds, finishing in dummy. His remaining cards are:

♠ A K Q 7 5
♡ 9
♦ —
♣ 8

♠ 8
♡ —
♦ —
♣ A K J 10 6 5

It is right to finesse in clubs now *because*, if East began with Qxxx (more likely than xxxx), West will assuredly be squeezed in the major suits when three rounds of clubs are cashed.

It may well be that Passell, with a sight of only 26 cards, saw more clearly than those who were looking at all 52.

37

Youthful Excess

With North the dealer, and playing a strong notrump, how do you think these two hands should be bid?

♠ A Q
♥ 9 4 2
♦ A 10 3
♣ Q 8 7 6 4

♠ 10 9 7 5 3
♥ A 10 6 5 3
♦ 7 5 2
♣ —

It is simple enough:

South	North
—	1♣
1♠	1 NT
2♥	No

It is unwise, in general, to raise the level of the auction on a bad hand, but over 1 NT two hearts is not forcing. North, of course, should be happy to pass two hearts; only a beginner would return to two spades.

But this is a type of hand on which players are liable to go too high. Jean Besse and Pierre Béguin admit that they did this themselves in their fairly distant youth. This was their sequence:

South	North
Besse	Béguin
—	1♣
1♠	1 NT
2♥	2 NT (a)
3♥ (b)	4♥ (c)

(a) According to most modern ideas, quite wrong.

(b) Quite wrong in any age. Time to lie down before worse befalls.

(c) Oddly enough, this is not unreasonable. If partner is 5–5, fair values, the North hand should be useful.

West led a club against four hearts and the declarer contemplated:

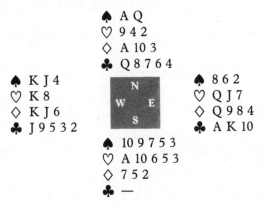

```
            ♠ A Q
            ♡ 9 4 2
            ◇ A 10 3
            ♣ Q 8 7 6 4
♠ K J 4                      ♠ 8 6 2
♡ K 8          N             ♡ Q J 7
◇ K J 6     W     E          ◇ Q 9 8 4
♣ J 9 5 3 2    S             ♣ A K 10
            ♠ 10 9 7 5 3
            ♡ A 10 6 5 3
            ◇ 7 5 2
            ♣ —
```

All went well. Club ruff, spade queen and ace, club ruff, spade ruff, club ruff, and these cards were left:

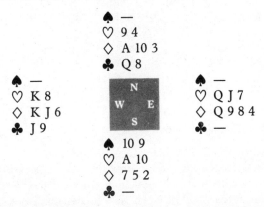

```
            ♠ —
            ♡ 9 4
            ◇ A 10 3
            ♣ Q 8
♠ —                          ♠ —
♡ K 8          N             ♡ Q J 7
◇ K J 6     W     E          ◇ Q 9 8 4
♣ J 9         S              ♣ —
            ♠ 10 9
            ♡ A 10
            ◇ 7 5 2
            ♣ —
```

South has only two tricks on top and needs four. Jean declaes that he can always make them. At the table he led a spade. West ruffed with the king and returned a heart to the jack and ace. Declarer crossed to the ace of diamonds and led the queen of clubs. Yes, that wins four tricks. What does it prove? Only that some players are luckier than others!

38

Third Choice

If odds interest you, what do you think are the chances for seven hearts on the deal below, ignoring the actual lie of the cards? Seven hearts is slightly better than seven spades, because if the spades are 4–0 you will never make seven spades but may make seven hearts.

Dealer West   Love all

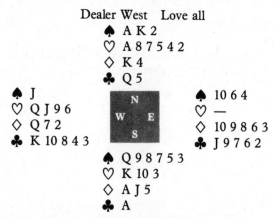

```
                 ♠ A K 2
                 ♡ A 8 7 5 4 2
                 ◇ K 4
                 ♣ Q 5
  ♠ J                          ♠ 10 6 4
  ♡ Q J 9 6                    ♡ —
  ◇ Q 7 2                      ◇ 10 9 8 6 3
  ♣ K 10 8 4 3                 ♣ J 9 7 6 2
                 ♠ Q 9 8 7 5 3
                 ♡ K 10 3
                 ◇ A J 5
                 ♣ A
```

The chances of a 2–2 break in hearts are (in theory) 40%, but a new calculation is needed when West drops the jack or queen on the first round. It is slightly better to play him for a singleton honour. The effect of this is that you lose when West holds a doubleton Q J, gain when he holds a singleton. This improves your prospects to 42%, but you have to deduct a little because of the possibility of spades being 4–0 and West leading a spade.

In a rubber bridge game North–South finished in a grand slam, but not in hearts and not spades! This was the sequence:

South	West	North	East
—	No	1♡	No
1♠	No	2♠	No
6♠(1)	No	7♠(2)	Dble(3)
7NT(4)	No	No	No

(1) Not everyone's choice, but by no means unreasonable.

(2) He had quite a bit in hand—important cards, too.

(3) East defended his double on the grounds that a heart lead might be essential to beat seven spades.

(4) It wasn't difficult to guess the reason for East's double.

West led his singleton spade against 7 NT. Assuming that West holds QJ9x of hearts, has South any chance?

After six rounds of spades and the ace of clubs the position was:

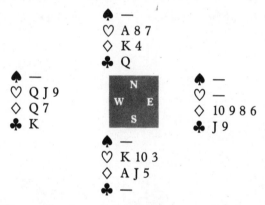

At this stage South was fairly confident that West held the hearts and the king of clubs. (East's double of seven spades must have been based on a void in hearts and if West had held long clubs headed by the J108 he would probably have led a club). A successful finesse in diamonds would lead to a simple squeeze, and this was really the odds play, because East had surely begun with more diamonds than his partner. But perhaps West had shown signs of discomfort, or perhaps South wanted to go down in the record books as the man who had picked up two tricks in a grand slam contract. At any rate, he banged out king and ace of diamonds, after which the jack of diamonds was more than West could bear.

39

Anything You Can Do . . .

I suppose it's often the way that when one reads the account of a long final one wonders how either team got past the first round. Study this deal from the final of the Spingold Trophy a few years ago. The event was contested by 129 of the best American and Canadian teams, all of them possessors of innumerable master points.

Dealer West   Love all

```
                    ♠ 5
                    ♡ 10
                    ◇ K J 7 5 4
                    ♣ A 10 9 7 4 2
     ♠ A 7                              ♠ K Q 6 3
     ♡ K 6 3 2          N               ♡ A Q J 4
     ◇ A Q 6 2      W       E           ◇ 10 8 3
     ♣ K 8 6            S               ♣ Q J
                    ♠ J 10 9 8 4 2
                    ♡ 9 8 7 5
                    ◇ 9
                    ♣ 5 3
```

This was the bidding at the first table:

South	West	North	East
Lair	Cohen	Andersen	Glubok
—	1 NT	2 NT (1)	No
3 ♣	No	No	Dble (2)
No	No	No	

(1) Ron Andersen is one of the world's top players, but really, what is the sense of this intervention over a strong notrump?

(2) Not an easy decision, by any means. The trump holding is unfavourable and game somewhere is very likely.

East's double turned out very well. West led a low club and the ace was played from dummy, followed by a low diamond. East went in with the 10, and the final result was five down, 900 (more now). 900 was not enough. At the other table:

South	West	North	East
Schermer	Goldman	Chambers	Soloway
—	1♦	2♣	Dble
No	3♡	No	4♡
4♠	Dble	No	No
No			

You can see what went through South's mind. When hearts were bid and supported it was certain that partner would be short, so he might well have spade support. At pairs, against vulnerable opponents, this might, just, lead to a small gain. At IMPs it was ridiculous; it cost 1100.

Reverting to the 'unusual notrump', practised at the first table, I venture to quote from *The Acol System of Bidding*, by Albert Dormer and myself:

'A point to bear in mind about the unusual notrump is that if opponents eventually buy the contract the declarer will have a valuable guide to the distribution of unseen hands. It is therefore unwise to brandish this toy except when you have a definite possibility of challenging for the contract. . . . If opponents have a misfit they will play for a penalty, and if instead they win the contract either in a suit or notrumps they will benefit considerably from the knowledge that one defender holds ten cards in the minor suits.'

40

Diamond Cut Diamond

The following deal is based on an idea of the fine American writer,
Eddie Kantar.

             ♠ A Q 4 3
             ♡ A K 8 6
             ◇ K Q 6 5 4
             ♣ —

♣ A led

             ♠ K 8 6 2
             ♡ Q 9 2
             ◇ A 8 7
             ♣ Q 7 2

Any of a hundred sequences would take North–South to the
obvious contract of six spades. West begins with a high club and
dummy ruffs. South cashes ace and queen of spades and visions of
an overtrick disappear when East discards a heart on the second
round.

The declarer might come to hand with a heart or a diamond and
ruff another club, but he will still have a third club and may not be
able to discard it before West ruffs the third round of diamonds or
the third round of hearts. It may seem a better plan, therefore, to
play on diamonds, allowing West to ruff while there is still a trump
in dummy. Let's see how that plan fares when the distribution is:

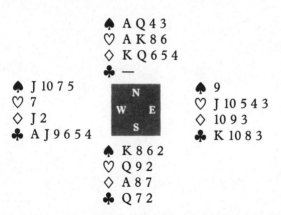

The play goes; club ruffed, ♠ AQ, ◇ AKQ. If West ruffs, all is well, but West is too clever: he doesn't ruff the third diamond, he discards his singleton heart. South disposes of a club on the fourth round of diamonds, but West ruffs and leads a club. Dummy can ruff this but South has no way way of returning to hand to draw the outstanding trump.

Will good defence always prevail, then? No, South was wrong to play A K Q of diamonds. He should cash K Q first. This is the situation when the third round is led:

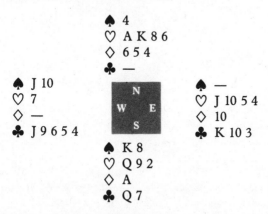

Again, West doesn't ruff the third round of diamonds—he discards his singleton heart. No matter, South ruffs a club and discards his remaining club on the fourth diamond. West may ruff when he pleases, but it is the only trick he will make.

41

Two Lovely Black Eyes

Edward Frischauer was one of the great Austrian players who won
the world championship at Budapest in 1937. He had the wit to
emigrate to America in 1938 and had a most successful career there,
both in property and in bridge. As a dummy player, he was
considered the equal of Karl Schneider. Just one card that he
played on the following deal would be enough to establish anyone's
reputation.

```
              Dealer South   Love all
                    ♠ K Q 2
                    ♡ A 8 5
                    ◇ A 10 3
                    ♣ 10 5 3 2
    ♡ 3 led
                    ♠ 3
                    ♡ K 7 2
                    ◇ 6 5
                    ♣ A K Q J 8 7 4
```

The bidding, in 1938, when bidding was fairly sensible, might
have been such as one club—3 NT—six clubs. At any rate, the
contract is six clubs and West leads the 3 of hearts.

If you are thinking deeply about the play, you haven't quite
caught up with the Austrian master. In a few seconds he had won
with the ace of hearts and had led the 2 of spades from dummy. See
the effect of that:

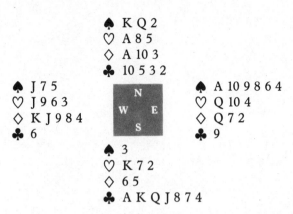

```
                    ♠ K Q 2
                    ♡ A 8 5
                    ◇ A 10 3
                    ♣ 10 5 3 2
    ♠ J 7 5                        ♠ A 10 9 8 6 4
    ♡ J 9 6 3          N           ♡ Q 10 4
    ◇ K J 9 8 4    W       E       ◇ Q 7 2
    ♣ 6                S            ♣ 9
                    ♠ 3
                    ♡ K 7 2
                    ◇ 6 5
                    ♣ A K Q J 8 7 4
```

There was virtually no hope of a squeeze and a spade from hand, even if West held the ace, would gain nothing, because a good player would not part with the ace (presenting declarer with two tricks in the suit if he had begun with a singleton). So Frischauer won the heart lead in dummy and advanced the 2 of spades. Poor East!

Half a century later the reverse of this trick was played by the French international, Patrick Sussel.

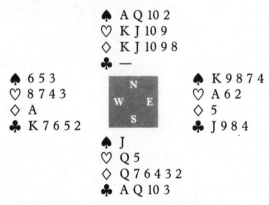

```
                    ♠ A Q 10 2
                    ♡ K J 10 9
                    ◇ K J 10 9 8
                    ♣ —
    ♠ 6 5 3                        ♠ K 9 8 7 4
    ♡ 8 7 4 3          N           ♡ A 6 2
    ◇ A            W       E       ◇ 5
    ♣ K 7 6 5 2        S            ♣ J 9 8 4
                    ♠ J
                    ♡ Q 5
                    ◇ Q 7 6 4 3 2
                    ♣ A Q 10 3
```

In a multiple team event this was the bidding:

South	West	North	East
—	—	—	No
1 ◇	No	1 ♡	1 ♠
No	2 ♠	6 ◇	No
No	No		

Two aces were missing, but you certainly can't blame North!

West led a low club. South ruffed in dummy and led—the 2 of spades! East ducked; you would have done the same. Now club ruff, ace and queen of spades, covered by East, club ruff, and the second heart was thrown on the 10 of spades. It was great play.

42

Place Your Bets

Where would you place your bets on this deal from a pairs event? North–South were vulnerable and the bidding was usually on these lines:

South	West	North	East
—	—	—	1♣
1♠	No	2♡	No
3♠	No	4♠	No
No	No		

And this was the full hand:

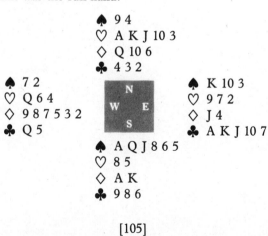

```
              ♠ 9 4
              ♡ A K J 10 3
              ◇ Q 10 6
              ♣ 4 3 2
♠ 7 2                        ♠ K 10 3
♡ Q 6 4          N           ♡ 9 7 2
◇ 9 8 7 5 3 2  W   E         ◇ J 4
♣ Q 5            S           ♣ A K J 10 7
              ♠ A Q J 8 6 5
              ♡ 8 5
              ◇ A K
              ♣ 9 8 6
```

If playing strong or intermediate jump overcalls, South might of course overcall with two spades. And there are those, heaven help us, who would think it appropriate to double.

The defence against four spades invariably began with three rounds of clubs. Should East try a fourth club now? Surely, for South must hold the ace of diamonds and it won't be difficult for him to pick up the trumps and discard any losing diamond on dummy's hearts. So East leads a fourth club. If he can persuade dummy to ruff, then his K 10 x of spades will be worth a trick.

When the fourth club is led it cannot be right for South to ruff with an honour. He has three other possibilities:

(1) He may discard and hope to win the trick with dummy's 9 of spades. This line will win if East has a doubleton K 10 of spades.
(2) He may ruff low, but this will make little difference to his chances.
(3) He does better to ruff with the 8 of spades. This holds, as the cards lie, and now East's K 10 x of spades can be picked up.

Was that your conclusion too? Sorry, but you have overlooked a small point. Clever West has discarded a heart on the third club and another heart on the fourth club. Now it is impossible for South to enter dummy twice to pick up East's trumps. You will not be surprised to learn that no-one found this defence at the table.

43

Getting Warm

Part scores at rubber bridge lead to situations that have no counterpart in the tournament game. Imagine that you are playing in four diamonds with the following cards:

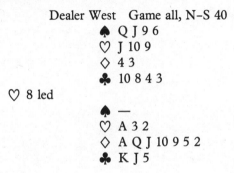

Dealer West   Game all, N–S 40

♠ Q J 9 6
♡ J 10 9
◇ 4 3
♣ 10 8 4 3

♡ 8 led

♠ —
♡ A 3 2
◇ A Q J 10 9 5 2
♣ K J 5

The bidding has been:

South	West	North	East
—	No	No	1♡
3◇	3♡	No	No
4◇	No	No	No

West's lead of the 8 of hearts is covered by the 9, queen and ace. Since West has supported hearts the suit is presumably breaking 4–3. In tournament play West would not have raised to the three level on three small; he would have passed or made one of the fashionable negative doubles. The raise is quite natural in a part score situation at rubber bridge. At any rate, you judge that it should be safe to establish a second trick in hearts, at the same time establishing an entry to dummy.

So you return a heart at trick two, which runs to the 10 and king. East now lays down the ace of clubs, on which his partner plays the 7, and follows with the 2 of clubs.

You might think for a moment of finessing, but if East held ♣ A Q x he would certainly not be giving you this chance, since dummy holds only one entry, the third round of hearts. It is reasonable to assume, therefore, that East holds a doubleton A x in clubs.

What of it, you may ask. You can win with the king of clubs, cross to the jack of hearts, and finesse the queen of diamonds. But would that be clever?

Think again. What is the likely distribution of the East hand? Presumably he has four hearts. You have placed him with a doubleton in clubs. (You may confirm this by playing a third round of clubs.) Can he hold five spades? Obviously not, for then he would have opened one spade, not one heart.

You are getting warm. He must hold *at least* three diamonds. The full hand was:

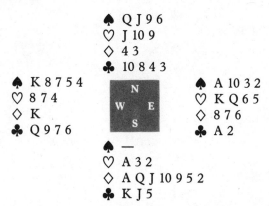

```
                    ♠ Q J 9 6
                    ♡ J 10 9
                    ◇ 4 3
                    ♣ 10 8 4 3
  ♠ K 8 7 5 4                        ♠ A 10 3 2
  ♡ 8 7 4            N               ♡ K Q 6 5
  ◇ K           W         E          ◇ 8 7 6
  ♣ Q 9 7 6          S               ♣ A 2
                    ♠ —
                    ♡ A 3 2
                    ◇ A Q J 10 9 5 2
                    ♣ K J 5
```

It just wasn't possible for East to hold a doubleton king of diamonds. The only chance was to go up with the ace of diamonds, hoping to bring down a singleton king.

44

Not Impressed

'I was in Stockholm recently', said a friend at the club. 'I met several of the top Swedish players, including Jan Wohlin'.

'Has he recovered from his accident?' someone asked. The Swedish 'Fat Boy' had set fire to himself in the traditional way, going to sleep and leaving a lighted cigarette.

'He seemed quite all right. He showed me one of his problems. Would you like to look at it?' He wrote it down:

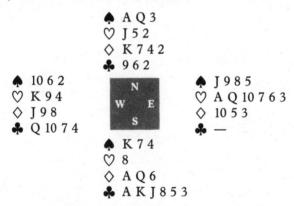

♠ A Q 3
♥ J 5 2
♦ K 7 4 2
♣ 9 6 2

♠ 10 6 2
♥ K 9 4
♦ J 9 8
♣ Q 10 7 4

♠ J 9 8 5
♥ A Q 10 7 6 3
♦ 10 5 3
♣ —

♠ K 7 4
♥ 8
♦ A Q 6
♣ A K J 8 5 3

'South plays in five clubs after East has overcalled in hearts. The defence begins with two rounds of hearts. You ruff and lay down the ace of clubs, on which East shows out.'

Not waiting for me to interpose my amateurish suggestion, he went on:

'I know I'm not an expert like some of you chaps, but this didn't seem very difficult to me. Cash three spades and three diamonds, ruff the third heart, and there you are, with a trump endplay.'

'Was Wohlin impressed?' I asked.

'Well, that was a bit funny. He had told me not to look at the East–West hands, and of course I didn't, though it wasn't easy. Typical of my luck—when I play a hand well they say I've looked at all the cards.'

I had had time by now to see the point of the problem. 'Perhaps he thought you'd played the hand too well', I suggested. 'There is another possibility, you know. Suppose the full hand had been:

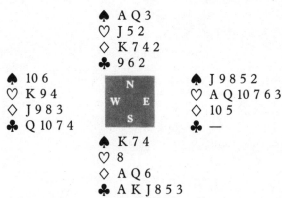

♠ A Q 3
♡ J 5 2
◇ K 7 4 2
♣ 9 6 2

♠ 10 6
♡ K 9 4
◇ J 9 8 3
♣ Q 10 7 4

♠ J 9 8 5 2
♡ A Q 10 7 6 3
◇ 10 5
♣ —

♠ K 7 4
♡ 8
◇ A Q 6
♣ A K J 8 5 3

'Now if you start with three rounds of spades you run into a ruff, don't you? It is better to play on diamonds first because you may then be able to cope when West has four diamonds and only two spades. When you find that West holds the long diamonds you can ruff the fourth round and cash just two spades, as his distribution has to be 2–3–4–4. You ruff the third heart and play the third round of spades, which he has to ruff.'

He was not in the least impressed. 'That's interesting in a way', was his comment. 'It means that you may make this contract even if you haven't got the queen of spades.'

45

Safety-Catch

Anyone—well, almost anyone—can knock out an ace from the dummy when obviously this card may be needed as as entry. To remove an inconspicuous entry in the trump suit before the declarer can make good use of it is a form of play that is often missed, even by good players.

Dealer West   N–S vulnerable

```
                    ♠ K 8 5 4 3
                    ♡ Q 10
                    ◇ 9
                    ♣ A 8 4 3 2
   ♠ Q J 10                          ♠ 2
   ♡ 9 4 2              N            ♡ 3
   ◇ A J 7 3        W     E          ◇ K Q 10 8 6 5 2
   ♣ Q 10 7            S             ♣ J 9 6 5
                    ♠ A 9 7 6
                    ♡ A K J 8 7 6 5
                    ◇ 4
                    ♣ K
```

After two passes East opened three diamonds and the bidding continued:

South	West	North	East
—	No	No	3 ◇
4 ♡	5 ◇	6 ♡	No
No	No		

West began with the ace of diamonds, on which East played the 2. The queen of spades looked safe at trick two; at least, it looked safe to West. South won with the ace, cashed the king of clubs, and entered dummy with a trump. He ruffed a low club, returned to the queen of hearts, and ruffed another club. He was now well placed:

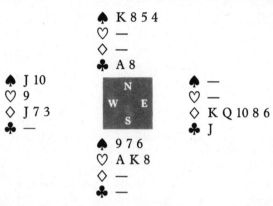

```
              ♠ K 8 5 4
              ♡ —
              ♢ —
              ♣ A 8
♠ J 10                        ♠ —
♡ 9                           ♡ —
♢ J 7 3                       ♢ K Q 10 8 6
♣ —                           ♣ J
              ♠ 9 7 6
              ♡ A K 8
              ♢ —
              ♣ —
```

After drawing the last trump declarer crossed to dummy and discarded two spades on the long clubs.

'He needed all those entries, didn't he?' said East. 'Isn't it better if you play a heart at trick two?'

'You played the 2 of diamonds on the first trick', West replied. 'I thought you might have held the ace of spades.'

'I played the 2 of diamonds to show an odd number', East persisted. 'Isn't that what the experts do nowadays? If I had wanted a spade I would have played the *queen* of diamonds. You had to play a heart on your hand. Then he can't get the long club going.'

46

Queen in Hiding

There are quite a few situations where a defender may achieve a mortal effect by holding up, or concealing, a trump honour. For example:

K J x

Q x x x   x

A 10 9 x

Suppose that North, who began with K J x x in the trump suit, has ruffed early on and that the declarer needs to keep general control. He leads the jack from dummy and runs it. If West wins there may be no defence, but if West holds up the queen South will probably follow with the king from dummy. The subsequent play may then be very awkward for him.

A defender with K J of the trump suit may gain by taking an early trick with the king. This position is fairly well known:

Q 9 8

x x x   K J x

A 10 x x

South leads low to the 9. If East wins with the jack his king will be picked up later, but if he wins the first trick with the king he may make another trick with the jack.

This deal from the match between Italy and Norway at Lausanne in 1979 shows a surprising variation:

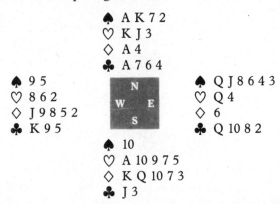

```
              ♠ A K 7 2
              ♡ K J 3
              ◇ A 4
              ♣ A 7 6 4
♠ 9 5                          ♠ Q J 8 6 4 3
♡ 8 6 2          N             ♡ Q 4
◇ J 9 8 5 2   W     E          ◇ 6
♣ K 9 5          S             ♣ Q 10 8 2
              ♠ 10
              ♡ A 10 9 7 5
              ◇ K Q 10 7 3
              ♣ J 3
```

Garozzo and Lauria played in six hearts after East had overcalled in spades. West led a spade, won in dummy. Obviously South must attend to the side suit before drawing trumps, so at trick two Garozzo led the ace of diamonds from dummy and followed with a second diamond. It might have turned out well for the defence if East had ruffed this, but usually it is wrong to ruff a loser and East in practice discarded a spade. Declarer won with ◇ K and ruffed a low diamond with ♡ J. East overruffed and from then on there was no defence, as the other diamond loser was ruffed by the king of hearts.

Now just suppose that East had declined to overruff the jack of hearts. South would have discarded a club on the king of spades, ruffed a club, and ruffed a diamond with the king of hearts. It would have looked right then to play ace and 10 of hearts. To the declarer's surprise, East would produce the queen and this would be the position:

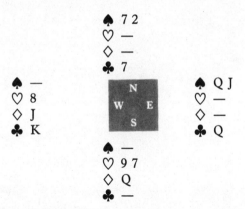

```
                ♠ 7 2
                ♡ —
                ◇ —
                ♣ 7
    ♠ —                          ♠ Q J
    ♡ 8         N                ♡ —
    ◇ J      W     E             ◇ —
    ♣ K         S                ♣ Q
                ♠ —
                ♡ 9 7
                ◇ Q
                ♣ —
```

Now a spade from East promotes his partner's 8 of hearts. All this is difficult for East to foresee, of course, but the general stratagem of concealing a trump honour (which is sure to make eventually) may one day win you a prize.

47

No Dissenting Voice

At the end of the world championship at Copacabana, in Brazil,
Jean Besse was asked to name the winner of the Brilliancy award. I
dare say he didn't find the decision too difficult. This was deal 20 of
the match between Italy and the United States.

Dealer South   Game all

At both tables South played in 3 NT and West began with a low
club. There are eight tricks on top, evidently: five diamonds, ace of
spades, and two clubs after the ace has been forced out.

At the first table Franco, for Italy, ran the jack of hearts at trick
two. West won with the queen and led a second low club. Now the
defenders were in control.

At the other table Passell sought his ninth trick in spades, which
seems to be better play. In dummy with the king of clubs, he
crossed to the ace of spades, played a diamond to dummy, and
advanced the queen of spades.

'He's going to make it now', declared the commentators, Kaplan and Besse, and no-one disputed this. But Garozzo (who could see only 26 cards, not 52 like the bridgerama audience) had a different idea. This was the position after he had won with the king of spades:

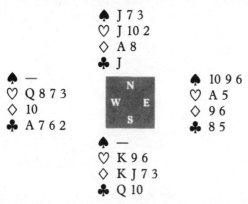

```
                  ♠ J 7 3
                  ♡ J 10 2
                  ◇ A 8
                  ♣ J
   ♠ —                          ♠ 10 9 6
   ♡ Q 8 7 3          N         ♡ A 5
   ◇ 10            W     E      ◇ 9 6
   ♣ A 7 6 2          S         ♣ 8 5
                  ♠ —
                  ♡ K 9 6
                  ◇ K J 7 3
                  ♣ Q 10
```

Like a player in a chess problem who makes an apparently harmless, but in fact devastating, move, Benito led the 6 of diamonds. Declarer won with the ace in dummy but was now in a quandary. If he plays the jack of spades (as he did), he sets up five winners for the defence. If he plays a heart East can take the ace and play a second round (South having discarded a heart on the second round of spades). And if he plays a club, West can win and return a club, leaving the declarer in his own hand with three losers.

The principle underlying East's lead of a diamond is one of the most elusive in the game. When the declarer has nine tricks in view but needs (a) to cash a winner (the jack of spades), and (b) to establish a winner (in clubs), the best line of attack may be the suit (diamonds) which he needs for transportation.

48

Cut the Line

On the first deal of a new rubber the player in West's position picked up:

> ♠ J 10 9 8 6 2
> ♡ —
> ◇ K 6 5 4
> ♣ A 9 8

South opened one heart and the bidding continued:

South	West	North	East
1♡	1♠	2♠	4◇
No	?		

What on earth does four diamonds mean, West asked herself. Has he got a string of diamonds or is he intending to support spades? I think I'll pass and see what happens next.

What happened next was that North bid six hearts, and this was followed by two passes. I'm not going to save against that, West decided, but what am I supposed to lead? North has shown control of spades and he can't be afraid of diamonds. I'll think I'll lead the ace of clubs and if that wins I can decide what to do after I've seen the dummy.

The ace of clubs was not a great success, the full hand being:

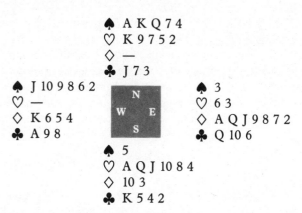

'What a lead!' exclaimed East after South had discarded two clubs on dummy's top spades. 'Didn't you hear me bid four diamonds? What's wrong with a low diamond?'

'Plenty', said South, who was the best player at the table. 'I ruff the two diamonds and play off all the trumps, reaching this position:

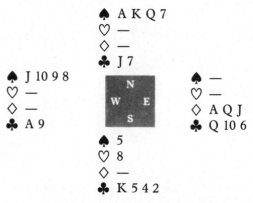

'What does West throw on the last heart? It's a squeeze without the count'.

'Exactly', said West virtuously. 'I knew a diamond lead wouldn't help'.

'Then you should lead a spade', said her partner. 'That breaks up any squeeze.'

This was true, but how could West know? She couldn't, but a spade lead still seems the best chance. The ace of clubs was far too likely to give away a vital trick, and certainly the opponents must be prepared for a diamond lead. A spade, on the other hand, might have an effect on the entry situation, cutting communications.

49

Under the Gun

The declarer who played the deal below was annoyed with himself for a rather strange reason. He made his contract with a form of *coup en passant* but was disappointed because he had missed the chance for a much more exotic play—the Devil's Coup, which is a form of smother play.

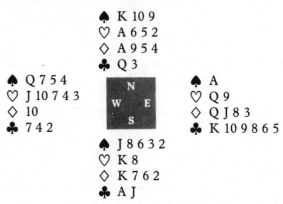

```
              ♠ K 10 9
              ♡ A 6 5 2
              ◇ A 9 5 4
              ♣ Q 3
♠ Q 7 5 4                      ♠ A
♡ J 10 7 4 3        N          ♡ Q 9
◇ 10           W        E      ◇ Q J 8 3
♣ 7 4 2             S          ♣ K 10 9 8 6 5
              ♠ J 8 6 3 2
              ♡ K 8
              ◇ K 7 6 2
              ♣ A J
```

As he was playing a strong notrump throughout, North opened one diamond and the bidding continued:

South	West	North	East
—	—	1◇	2♣
2♠	No	3♠	No
4♠	No	No	No

West led a low club to the queen, king and ace. East won the first round of trumps and returned a club. On a spade to the 10 East showed out.

South can afford to lose two spades and a diamond, so his next move was a diamond to the king and a diamond from hand. West, obviously, was not going to ruff a loser, so he discarded a heart. Now there were two diamond losers, so a little thought was required.

It was not difficult to count West for four spades, one diamond, three clubs and therefore five hearts. Planning to make tricks with his low trumps, South played three rounds of hearts, ruffing in hand. The position was now:

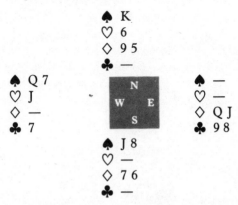

```
                    ♠ K
                    ♡ 6
                    ◇ 9 5
                    ♣ —
    ♠ Q 7                        ♠ —
    ♡ J              N           ♡ —
    ◇ —          W     E         ◇ Q J
    ♣ 7              S           ♣ 9 8
                    ♠ J 8
                    ♡ —
                    ◇ 7 6
                    ♣ —
```

With a small flourish South played a spade to the king and scored his tenth trick by ruffing the fourth heart with the jack of spades 'under the gun'.

The other players were surprised when South, ignoring muttered congratulations, uttered a loud cry. 'I could have played a Devil's Coup at the finish', he exclaimed. 'All I had to do was exit with a diamond. East makes his two diamond tricks, then leads a club, which I ruff with the 8. West's queen of spades is trapped.'

Yes. This form of smother play is described in all the books on advanced play, but how often does one see it at the table?

50

Nil Desperandum

To find the trumps 5–0 after you have opened on sub-minimum values is usually a hefty blow. South managed to survive on this occasion, when he and his partner held:

                    ♠ A K Q 5
                    ♡ A 3
                    ◇ 8 6
                    ♣ A K 8 7 2
    ♡ K led
                    ♠ 10 7 4 3
                    ♡ 7 6
                    ◇ A K Q 10 7
                    ♣ 10 4

At love all South opened one diamond. 'May stop the opponents from bidding and making 3NT' is the theory. West overcalled with three hearts and the bidding continued:

South	West	North	East
1◇	3♡	4♡ (1)	No
4♠	No	4NT	No
5◇	No	5NT	No
6◇	No	6♠ (2)	No
No	No		

(1) Most players would have done the same, but this type of call is always foolish when you don't know which way you are going. Four clubs would surely be forcing.
(2) South was lucky that his partner did not bid the grand slam.

West led the king of hearts and the blow fell at trick two when West did not follow to the ace of spades. Not quite sure what he was doing, South cashed two clubs and three diamonds. All followed, since this was the full hand.

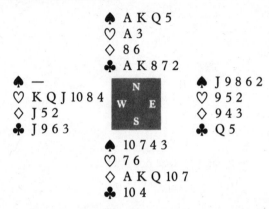

```
                 ♠ A K Q 5
                 ♡ A 3
                 ◇ 8 6
                 ♣ A K 8 7 2
♠ —                              ♠ J 9 8 6 2
♡ K Q J 10 8 4                   ♡ 9 5 2
◇ J 5 2                          ◇ 9 4 3
♣ J 9 6 3                        ♣ Q 5
                 ♠ 10 7 4 3
                 ♡ 7 6
                 ◇ A K Q 10 7
                 ♣ 10 4
```

After one heart, one spade, five minor suit winners and a heart ruff, the position was:

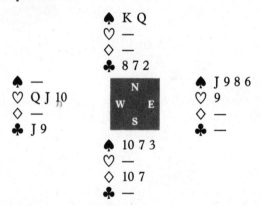

```
                 ♠ K Q
                 ♡ —
                 ◇ —
                 ♣ 8 7 2
♠ —                              ♠ J 9 8 6
♡ Q J 10                         ♡ 9
◇ —                              ◇ —
♣ J 9                            ♣ —
                 ♠ 10 7 3
                 ♡ —
                 ◇ 10 7
                 ♣ —
```

Declarer leads a club from the table. Now there are three possibilities:
(1) East discards. South ruffs, trumps a diamond high, and may now cash the second spade or lead another club.

(2) East ruffs the first club with the spade jack and returns a trump. Now a club is led from dummy and if East ruffs declarer can overruff and make the last two tricks with a spade and the fifth club.

(3) At the table East ruffed dummy's club with the 8 of spades. South overruffed, played a spade to the queen, and led another club. What can East do? If he ruffs and plays a spade, dummy's last club is good, and if he exits with a heart South makes the last two tricks on a crossruff.

51

Patience is a Virtue

Both sides had an opportunity for good play on this deal from a team event. Let's consider, first, the declarer's play in six spades.

```
              ♠ K 9 3
              ♡ 8 6 4
              ◇ A Q
              ♣ J 10 9 8 5
◇ 8 led
              ♠ A Q J 10 7 4
              ♡ A J 5 3 2
              ◇ 3
              ♣ A
```

At love all the bidding has been:

South	West	North	East
1♠	2◇	3♠	No
6♠	No	No	No

West leads the 8 of diamonds. No-one could criticise the bidding; the fit, or non-fit, in hearts is unfortunate.

There are some possible ways of holding the heart losers to one. You could play East for the K Q, or you might lay down the ace, gaining when West held a singleton king or queen. The declarer thought of another line: he finessed the queen of diamonds (likely to hold after West's overcall), then discarded the ace of clubs on dummy's ace of diamonds. He planned to find the club honours divided and to set up enough winners to dispose of his heart losers. The lie of the cards seems to favour this plan.

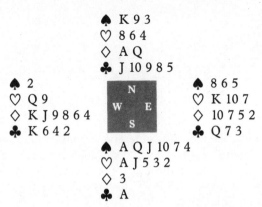

```
              ♠ K 9 3
              ♡ 8 6 4
              ◇ A Q
              ♣ J 10 9 8 5
♠ 2                            ♠ 8 6 5
♡ Q 9          N               ♡ K 10 7
◇ K J 9 8 6 4  W   E           ◇ 10 7 5 2
♣ K 6 4 2          S           ♣ Q 7 3
              ♠ A Q J 10 7 4
              ♡ A J 5 3 2
              ◇ 3
              ♣ A
```

After throwing the ace of clubs on the second round of diamonds, South ran the jack of clubs to West's king. After two rounds of trumps he took the ruffing finesse in clubs. This left:

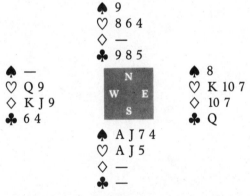

```
              ♠ 9
              ♡ 8 6 4
              ◇ —
              ♣ 9 8 5
♠ —                            ♠ 8
♡ Q 9          N               ♡ K 10 7
◇ K J 9        W   E           ◇ 10 7
♣ 6 4              S           ♣ Q
              ♠ A J 7 4
              ♡ A J 5
              ◇ —
              ♣ —
```

When East followed to the next club South was able to ruff high, play a spade to the 9, and dispose of two more hearts.

An unusual form of defence would have beaten the contract. West must not take the king of clubs on the first round of the suit. On the second round East will probably play the queen, forcing South to ruff. After two rounds of trumps the declarer may run another club to West's king, but now a fourth club is ruffed by East and South is a trick short.

The play would be essentially the same if East contributed his queen on the first round of clubs. Again, West must not take his king until the third round.

No Time for Despair

In the days when governesses were a normal part of the household there was a continual risk of being told, 'You're so sharp you'll cut yourself'. This admonition might have been addressed to the West player on a celebrated deal from the semi-final of the Canadian team championship in 1987.

Dealer South   E–W vulnerable

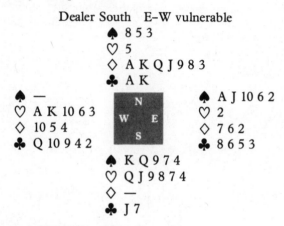

```
                 ♠ 8 5 3
                 ♡ 5
                 ◇ A K Q J 9 8 3
                 ♣ A K
  ♠ —                          ♠ A J 10 6 2
  ♡ A K 10 6 3                 ♡ 2
  ◇ 10 5 4                     ◇ 7 6 2
  ♣ Q 10 9 4 2                 ♣ 8 6 5 3
                 ♠ K Q 9 7 4
                 ♡ Q J 9 8 7 4
                 ◇ —
                 ♣ J 7
```

This was the bidding at the first table:

South	West	North	East
1♠	2♠ (1)	4NT	No
5◇ (2)	No	6◇	No
No	No		

(1) Denoting hearts and a minor. As I expect I have remarked elsewhere, I think these distributional bids on weak hands are extremely foolish.

(2) To treat a void as an ace—if that is what he was doing —is dangerous at this level; still more so when you have opened light.

What do you think happened in this slam with two aces missing? Right, West began with the 3 of hearts and North's 5 won the first trick. So the slam was made.

What do you think of West's lead? Since he held defensive tricks in hearts and clubs, and there was a fair chance that partner would hold something in spades, it was (like his bidding) extremely foolish. It was certainly not the moment for a desperation lead.

At the other table, also, the West player did not distinguish himself. The bidding went:

South	West	North	East
1♠	No	3♢	No
3♡	No	4♢	No
4♡	Dble(1)	4NT	No
5♢	No	No(2)	No

(1) So silly to double at this point! If the hand is to be played in diamonds you want partner to lead an unbid suit.
(2) This North, apparently, did not read his partner for an ace.

East led a heart, naturally, and the contract could not then be defeated.

If West had not doubled four hearts, could East have found the lead of the ace of spades? Le Dentu, in the French magazine, remarked that players seldom force these days when they are very short in partner's suit. Thus East might well have placed his partner with a singleton spade, if not a void.

53

Emergency Call

Many of the oldest ideas about squeeze play had to be revised when the Hungarian writer, Géza Ottlik, wrote a series of articles for the American *Bridge World* and when later he combined with Hugh Kelsey in a book entitled *Adventures in Card Play*. Study this miniature jewel:

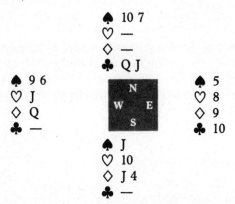

Spades are trumps and the lead is in dummy. Can declarer make all the tricks? You will need to look at it twice before you see the play: queen of clubs ruffed by the jack of spades and West discards . . . what?

It would be wrong to assume that this was some kind of freakish ending that would never occur at the table. This, after all, is a very ordinary-looking deal:

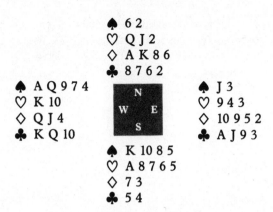

Against vulnerable opponents North decides to open one diamond—well, that's the story. The bidding then proceeds:

South	West	North	East
—	—	1◇	No
1♡	1♠	No	No
1NT	Dble	2♡	No
No	No		

West leads the king of clubs. East overtakes and returns the jack of spades, which is covered by the king and ace. West cashes the queen of spades and follows with two more rounds of clubs, South ruffing. A low heart is won by the king and a heart is returned. The position is now:

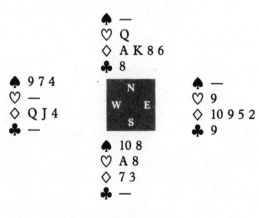

If South were in his own hand there would be no problem. As it is, he plays three rounds of diamonds, ruffing the third, then ruffs the 8 of spades with the queen of hearts. East, down to 999, is miraculously squeezed.

54

Exercise in Control

During the years when Italy was on top of the world Belladonna and Avarelli, Forquet and Garozzo, stole most of the headlines. So it is pleasant to record a deal played by Vito Pittala during the qualifying round of the 1975 Bermuda Bowl.

Dealer North   N–S vulnerable

```
              ♠ 10 9 6 5 3 2
              ♡ 6
              ◇ J 10 6
              ♣ J 5 2
♠ K Q J 8 4                    ♠ 7
♡ 10 5              N          ♡ A 9 3 2
◇ 8 7 5 3      W       E       ◇ K Q 9
♣ 10 3             S          ♣ K 8 7 6 4
              ♠ A
              ♡ K Q J 8 7 4
              ◇ A 4 2
              ♣ A Q 9
```

The Italians were North–South, playing against France. This was the bidding:

South	West	North	East
Pittala	Boulenger	Franco	Svarc
—	—	No	1♣
No(1)	1♠	No	2♣
4♡(2)	No	No	No

[133]

(1) I don't suppose one club was forcing, but probably, if West had passed, North would have been obliged in the system to reopen. (It seems to me a silly arrangement, but that's another matter.)

(2) There was not much else he could do now.

South was hoping for a club lead, no doubt, but West began with the king of spades. When the king and queen of hearts were allowed to hold, declarer played a third round. East cashed two heart tricks and exited with a club. After two rounds of clubs and one more trump the position was:

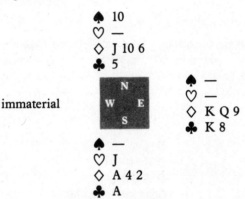

immaterial

Now Pittala led his last trump, discarding the spade from dummy. What do you want East to do? If he throws a diamond, declarer plays ace and another; if a club, then the ace is cashed and a low diamond follows.

Note that it would have been a mistake for South to cash the ace of clubs before leading the trump winners. This would have allowed East to keep ◇ K Q and ♣ K and make two of the last three tricks.

At the other table the French stopped in three hearts, just made, so it was 10 IMPs to Italy.

55

Hold Your Fire (1)

The chess maestro, Bobby Fischer, once wrote: 'You have thought of a good move. Bravo! But don't be hasty. There may well be a better move.'

The same advice holds good for bridge, especially in the broad area of overruffing. A comparative novice learns quite soon that with K 10 x sitting over the declarer's A Q J x x x it is good play not to overruff the queen. This is a much less obvious situation:

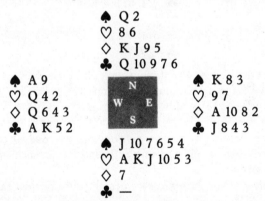

```
              ♠ Q 2
              ♡ 8 6
              ◇ K J 9 5
              ♣ Q 10 9 7 6
  ♠ A 9                        ♠ K 8 3
  ♡ Q 4 2          N           ♡ 9 7
  ◇ Q 6 4 3    W     E         ◇ A 10 8 2
  ♣ A K 5 2        S           ♣ J 8 4 3
              ♠ J 10 7 6 5 4
              ♡ A K J 10 5 3
              ◇ 7
              ♣ —
```

South, who has bid both majors, plays in four spades. He ruffs the club lead and sets about the hearts, ruffing the third round with the queen.

If East overruffs and plays a club, South can easily survive. He ruffs, leads the jack of spades, ruffs the return, and draws the remaining trumps with the 10 of spades. He even has a trump to spare.

It's all very different if East declines to overruff the queen of spades. South does not lose control altogether, but he cannot escape the loss of three trump tricks.

The general idea of not overruffing when you have a useful trump holding is well understood nowadays. What is not so well known is that it is often wrong to overruff even with short trumps. (I remember, goodness knows how many years ago, holding A x of the trump suit over dummy's singleton queen. The declarer, Chiaradia, ruffed with the queen and I gained a trick by refusing to overruff.) Here South is in four spades after East has bid hearts:

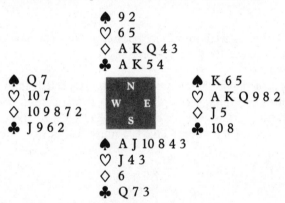

```
                  ♠ 9 2
                  ♡ 6 5
                  ◇ A K Q 4 3
                  ♣ A K 5 4
  ♠ Q 7                          ♠ K 6 5
  ♡ 10 7             N           ♡ A K Q 9 8 2
  ◇ 10 9 8 7 2   W     E         ◇ J 5
  ♣ J 9 6 2          S           ♣ 10 8
                  ♠ A J 10 8 4 3
                  ♡ J 4 3
                  ◇ 6
                  ♣ Q 7 3
```

The defence began with three rounds of hearts. It is tempting, perhaps, for West to make sure of a trump trick by ruffing with the queen of spades in front of dummy's 9. But if he does this it will be the end of the defence.

West does better, obviously—well, obviously if you look at all the cards—not to ruff at all. Dummy ruffs and the defence will then make two trump tricks.

More plays of the same kind are described in the next example.

56

Hold Your Fire (2)

The four hands below are almost exactly the same as in the last diagram. The main difference is that West now holds J x of spades instead of Q x. Again the contract is four spades and the defence begins with a heart to the king, ace of hearts and a third round.

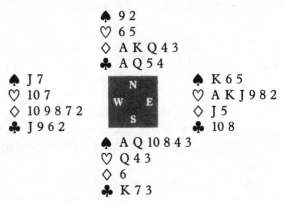

```
                    ♠ 9 2
                    ♡ 6 5
                    ◇ A K Q 4 3
                    ♣ A Q 5 4
    ♠ J 7                         ♠ K 6 5
    ♡ 10 7            N           ♡ A K J 9 8 2
    ◇ 10 9 8 7 2   W     E        ◇ J 5
    ♣ J 9 6 2         S           ♣ 10 8
                    ♠ A Q 10 8 4 3
                    ♡ Q 4 3
                    ◇ 6
                    ♣ K 7 3
```

The question is, what should West play on the third round of hearts? He could ruff with the jack of spades, he could ruff with the 7 of spades, or he could discard, since evidently the discard on the queen of hearts will not be of any use to the declarer.

It's not easy to see at once that the best play—the only play that gives the defence a chance to make two trump tricks—is to ruff with the 7 of spades. The likelihood now is that South will overruff with the 9 and finesse the 10 on the next round, as he will expect this to win or to force the king from West. To finesse the queen would lose if West had begun with K x.

Here is another tricky hand where a defender who has an obvious opportunity to overruff must decline to do so:

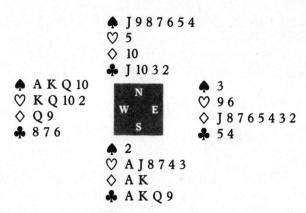

♠ J 9 8 7 6 5 4
♥ 5
♦ 10
♣ J 10 3 2

♠ A K Q 10
♥ K Q 10 2
♦ Q 9
♣ 8 7 6

♠ 3
♥ 9 6
♦ J 8 7 6 5 4 3 2
♣ 5 4

♠ 2
♥ A J 8 7 4 3
♦ A K
♣ A K Q 9

South deals at game all and the bidding goes:

South	North
2♣	2♦
2♥	2♠
3♣	3♠
4♥	5♣
No	

East discards a heart on the second round of spades and South ruffs. Declarer cashes the ace of hearts, ruffs a heart high, returns to the ace of diamonds and ruffs a third heart. After a trump to the ace the position is:

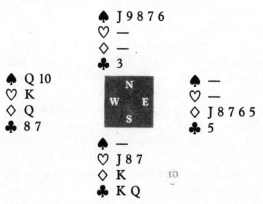

♠ J 9 8 7 6
♥ —
♦ —
♣ 3

♠ Q 10
♥ K
♦ Q
♣ 8 7

♠ —
♥ —
♦ J 8 7 6 5
♣ 5

♠ —
♥ J 8 7
♦ K
♣ K Q

South ruffs a heart with dummy's 3 of clubs—and East must *not* overruff.

The deals described in the last two features won a prize for Jean Besse in one of the Bols competitions.

57

Night School

'That's the first rubber I've won all night', remarked the South player, entering 1460 on the scoresheet. 'And I don't think I've made a single mistake.'

'You don't?' said West. 'I'm not sure about this last hand, for one. Let's take another look at it.'

```
              ♠ A K 6 4 2
              ♡ K 8 7 6
              ◇ J 6
              ♣ K 10
  ♠ J 7 3                      ♠ 9 8 5
  ♡ Q 10          N            ♡ J 2
  ◇ K Q 9 5 4   W   E          ◇ 8 7
  ♣ J 9 4          S           ♣ Q 8 6 5 3 2
              ♠ Q 10
              ♡ A 9 5 4 3
              ◇ A 10 3 2
              ♣ A 7
```

North was the dealer and the bidding unimpressive:

South	North
—	1♠
2♡	4♡
4NT	5◇
6♡	No

South's 4NT was pointless. He intended to finish in six hearts, no more, no less, whatever the response.

West led the king of diamonds. South won, cashed king and ace of hearts, and made seven when the spades broke as well.

'So I played it badly?' South exclaimed. 'You would have made one more, I suppose?'

'Yes, you did play it badly,' West persisted. 'What would you have done if the hearts had broken 3–1?'

'I would have had to play to discard my diamond losers on the spades, I suppose,' said South, with diminishing confidence.

'You suppose? Even with the spades 3–3 you can't dispose of your diamond losers in time. Let's reconstruct the hand a little, giving East three hearts and four spades.

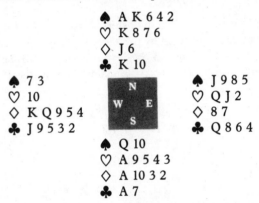

```
              ♠ A K 6 4 2
              ♡ K 8 7 6
              ◇ J 6
              ♣ K 10
 ♠ 7 3                        ♠ J 9 8 5
 ♡ 10              N          ♡ Q J 2
 ◇ K Q 9 5 4   W     E        ◇ 8 7
 ♣ J 9 5 3 2      S           ♣ Q 8 6 4
              ♠ Q 10
              ♡ A 9 5 4 3
              ◇ A 10 3 2
              ♣ A 7
```

'You began with king and ace of hearts, remember?' West continued. 'If they don't break you have no chance, whether the spades are 4–2 or 3–3. You can't get the diamond losers away in time. You must begin with ace and king of hearts, in that order. When they don't break your only chance is to finesse the 10 of spades, hoping to find East with Jxxx. As the cards lie in this diagram, you cash the 10 and queen of spades, cross to a club, and dispose of three diamond losers while East ruffs.'

'Incidentally,' West went on, 'whenever you need five tricks from this spade combination, the best line is to finesse the 10. This gains when East holds Jx or Jxxx, loses only when he holds xxx.'

'Here endeth the first lesson', said his opponent sourly.

58

Brighton Rock

In the 1987 European Championship, played at Brighton, the British team was slaughtered by the winners, Sweden. A couple of months later Britain reversed the result in the semi-final of the world championship. This was the main shock in the Brighton event:

Love all   Dealer West

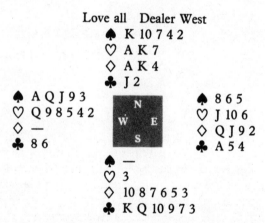

♠ K 10 7 4 2
♡ A K 7
◇ A K 4
♣ J 2

♠ A Q J 9 3
♡ Q 9 8 5 4 2
◇ —
♣ 8 6

♠ 8 6 5
♡ J 10 6
◇ Q J 9 2
♣ A 5 4

♠ —
♡ 3
◇ 10 8 7 6 5 3
♣ K Q 10 9 7 3

This was the sequence when Britain was East–West:

South	West	North	East
Göthe	Sheehan	Gullberg	Flint
—	1♠	1NT	2♠ (1)
5♣	5♡ (2)	Dble	5♠ (3)
No	No	Dble	No
No	No		

(1) East-West were playing five-card majors, but this bid still looks unnatural. For me, the choice would be between double and pass.

(2) Well, yes, he is 6–5, but any contract at the five level is going to cost 300 or more—and the opponents haven't made five clubs yet.

(3) Another poor call. It is quite likely that partner will have longer hearts than spades; anyway, you can pass and leave it to him.

The result of these errors was that West, forced at trick one and never able to draw trumps, made only six tricks yielding 1100.

The British pair at the other table was lucky or unlucky, as you choose to look at it.

South	West	North	East
Brock	Sundelin	Forrester	Flodqvist
—	No	1♠	No
1NT(1)	2♡	Dble	No
3♡(2)	No	3NT	No
4♣	No	4♢	No
4NT	No	5♣(3)	No
No	No		

(1) An awkward hand on any system. Pass, two clubs, two diamonds—none of them is satisfactory.

(2) Attempting to give a picture of his minor two-suiter.

(3) A bit exhausted by this time, I dare say.

Five clubs, as you can see, goes one down—or does it? South won the heart lead in dummy, ran the jack of clubs, and led another club, taken by the ace. Now East, understandably puzzled by the whole affair, led the queen of diamonds, so Brock made his contract. I imagine the Swedes were somewhat dismayed—until they discovered that they had gained 12 match points on the deal.

59

Jamaican Rum

When the 1987 world championship was played at Ocho Rios, in Jamaica, there was a peculiar arrangement whereby the American champions and the European winners, Sweden, were exempted till the semi-final, where they were opposed by teams that had been competing fiercely for almost a week. Whether this would favour the teams that were fresh or the teams that were 'played in' was open to question, and the question was not settled by the results of the semi-final matches. The team from Taiwan that had played so well in the qualifying round played below form against the Americans, but the British team easily revenged its defeat by Sweden in the European event. (The final was closely contested, the USA drawing away at the finish.)

This was the decisive deal in the match between Britain and Sweden:

Dealer East   Game all

                    ♠ A K 8 5 4
                    ♡ Q J 10 2
                    ◇ Q 5
                    ♣ 10 3
    ♠ 10 6   ♠ Q 9 7 3 2
    ♡ 7 6 5   N   ♡ A K 9 8 4
    ◇ A K 7 3   W   E   ◇ 2
    ♣ A 7 6 4   S   ♣ J 9
                    ♠ J
                    ♡ 3
                    ◇ J 10 9 8 6 4
                    ♣ K Q 8 5 2

When Sweden was North–South the bidding followed this remarkable course:

South	West	North	East
Fallenius	Forrester	Lindkvist	Armstrong
—	—	—	2NT(1)
No	3♡(2)	No	No
3NT(3)	Dble	No	No
Redble(4)	No	No(5)	No

(1) This denoted a moderate two-suiter, excluding clubs.
(2) If partner's suits are spades and diamonds they will finish in diamonds.
(3) Signifying intention to compete in a minor.
(4) Since partner had not expressed a preference, South would surely have been wiser to name his long suit, diamonds.
(5) Another bad call. In view of the strength of his own hand, not to mention West's double of 3NT, North should have realised that his partner was weak.

West led ♡5 to the 10 and king. East returned the 9, which was allowed to hold. Now East led ♣9 and South mistakenly played the king, which also was allowed to hold. When East came in later with ♡A he led ♣J . . . and it's all too terrible to describe. Britain scored 2800 in this room, less 140 at the other table, a swing of 21 match points.

From this deal, and the one preceding, the reader might suppose that the bidding and play in these championships was very uneven.That would be quite a wrong conclusion. When players are allowed to use *any* bidding system, as they were in these events, the game becomes much more tiring than usual . . . and occasionally it shows.

60

Ingenious Explanation

'Players are funny', a tournament director remarked to me. 'I was called to the table after this deal had been played. One of the defenders wanted to claim a foul on the grounds that North's two clubs was not a proper Stayman type.'

Dealer South   N–S vulnerable

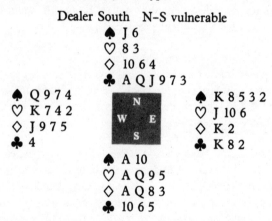

```
                    ♠ J 6
                    ♡ 8 3
                    ◇ 10 6 4
                    ♣ A Q J 9 7 3
    ♠ Q 9 7 4                        ♠ K 8 5 3 2
    ♡ K 7 4 2          N             ♡ J 10 6
    ◇ J 9 7 5      W       E         ◇ K 2
    ♣ 4                S             ♣ K 8 2
                    ♠ A 10
                    ♡ A Q 9 5
                    ◇ A Q 8 3
                    ♣ 10 6 5
```

North–South bid as follows:

South	North
1 NT	2♣
2♡	3 NT
No	

Since North had bid two clubs and then 3 NT over two hearts, West concluded that the responder was interested in spades. He led a diamond and now South had nine easy tricks.

To respond two clubs on the North hand is, of course, completely legal. As a tactical move, it may turn out badly if South, 4–4 in the majors, bids two hearts and then, over 3 NT, four spades. (It is easy to escape this hazard by devising a conventional sequence, such as 1 NT–2♣–3♢, to be used by an opener who holds both majors.)

The North player, if his explanation is to be believed, made a clever tactical bid on the following hand:

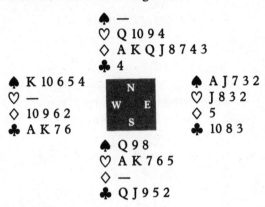

```
                    ♠ —
                    ♡ Q 10 9 4
                    ◇ A K Q J 8 7 4 3
                    ♣ 4
    ♠ K 10 6 5 4                      ♠ A J 7 3 2
    ♡ —              N                 ♡ J 8 3 2
    ◇ 10 9 6 2    W     E              ◇ 5
    ♣ A K 7 6        S                 ♣ 10 8 3
                    ♠ Q 9 8
                    ♡ A K 7 6 5
                    ◇ —
                    ♣ Q J 9 5 2
```

The bidding went:

South	West	North	East
1♡	Dble	Redble	1♠
2♣	3♠	6♢	No
No	Dble	6♡	No
No	Dble	No	No
No			

West led the ace of clubs, followed by a spade. South ruffed in dummy, ran the 10 of hearts, and followed with a stream of diamonds. East was unable to make a trick.

'Why did you bid six diamonds?' South wanted to know.

'I knew West would double if he was void of hearts', North replied. 'Then I would transfer to hearts and you would know how to play the trump suit.'

61

Dead Wood

Would you give South any chance in five spades on the deal below? On a club lead it can go three down, and it looks as though in any event the defence will make two clubs and a spade.

Dealer North Love all

```
                    ♠ K Q 3
                    ♡ 6 3
                    ◇ J 10 7 5 3
                    ♣ J 10 4
♠ 9 8 6                               ♠ A 2
♡ A K J 10 7 2                        ♡ Q 9 8 5 4
◇ —                                   ◇ K 9 2
♣ 9 7 6 5                             ♣ K Q 8
                    ♠ J 10 7 5 4
                    ♡ —
                    ◇ A Q 8 6 4
                    ♣ A 3 2
```

The bidding went:

South	West	North	East
—	—	No	1♡
1♠	4♡	4♠	No
No	5♡	No	No
5♠	No	No	Dble
No	No	No	

I don't know that I would have bid four spades on the North hand at equal vulnerability, but otherwise it was a well-judged auction. With the clubs lying so favourably, East would have made five hearts.

West led the ace of hearts against five spades doubled. South played a spade to the king and ace, and East, not wanting to give declarer a possible tempo by leading a diamond, returned a trump. South won in hand, played a third spade to dummy, and took the diamond finesse. A few tricks later the position was:

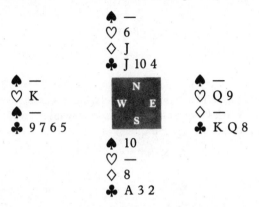

It was not too difficult to gauge the distribution. East had passed over North's four spades, so was likely to hold a fairly balanced distribution. When a diamond was led to dummy, East had to part with the 9 of hearts. Then a heart was ruffed and a low club left East on play; five made.

'If you'd led a diamond after the ace of spades I could have ruffed', said West, in the annoying way that some partners have.

'I suppose a heart would have defeated it, too', East reflected.

Yes, because then South has no trumps left in the endgame and East can come down to K Q of clubs and a heart winner. It was difficult to foresee that dummy's 6 of hearts would be an important card at the finish, but in general it is wise for defenders to remove the dead wood, not leaving any low cards around that may prove a threat later.

62

Two-Suiter Test

Supposing that you reached the fairly ambitious contract of six spades on the North–South hands below, how would you set about the play after West had led the queen of hearts?

♠ K 8 7
♡ A 7 6 5
♢ A J 6 5
♣ 3 2

♡ Q led

```
    N
 W     E
    S
```

♠ A 9 5 3 2
♡ K 4 3
♢ —
♣ A K J 5 4

You must assume, obviously, that the spades are going to break 3–2. The ace of diamonds will take care of your losing heart, so the question is, how are you going to manage the spades and clubs so that you will lose only the trump trick?

Many players—perhaps the majority—would cash ace and king of spades, then follow with three rounds of clubs. This works when the clubs are 3–3 and also when either defender holds Q x in clubs; but it will lose when the clubs are 4–2, with the queen in the long hand.

It is better play to tackle the clubs before the trumps. This became apparent when the deal was played, for this was the full hand:

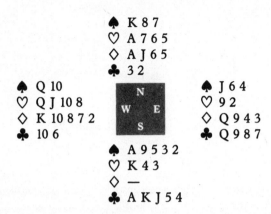

```
                    ♠ K 8 7
                    ♡ A 7 6 5
                    ◇ A J 6 5
                    ♣ 3 2
  ♠ Q 10                              ♠ J 6 4
  ♡ Q J 10 8         N                ♡ 9 2
  ◇ K 10 8 7 2     W   E              ◇ Q 9 4 3
  ♣ 10 6             S                ♣ Q 9 8 7
                    ♠ A 9 5 3 2
                    ♡ K 4 3
                    ◇ —
                    ♣ A K J 5 4
```

The declarer in six spades won the heart lead in dummy, then played ace, king and another club. West ruffed with the 10 of spades. It would be a mistake now to overruff, because after a spade to the ace and a ruff of the fourth club East would be left with J 6 of spades against South's 9 5.

After some thought the declarer came to this conclusion and discarded a diamond from dummy. He won the next heart, played a spade to the king, then finessed the 9 of spades, correctly playing West for Q 10 rather than Q J 10. Then he was able to ruff the fourth club and make the remainder.

It might have been better defence for West not to insert the 10 of spades on the third round of clubs. In this case South ruffs low, returns to hand with a diamond ruff, and advances the fourth club. West may ruff now, but again South declines to overruff. He picks up East's jack of spades in the same way as before and makes his contract.

It is a hand worth playing again in different ways, for these delicate two-suiters are quite common and are not easy to play.

63

Who Said 'Draw Trumps'?

At the end of a multi-team tournament I happened to overhear two
South players comparing notes about the following deal:

Dealer South   Game all

```
                    ♠ K 3
                    ♡ 10 8 5
                    ◇ J 10 4 3
                    ♣ A K 7 2
  ♠ 8 6 4 2                        ♠ 7
  ♡ K Q J 7          N             ♡ A 6 4 3 2
  ◇ Q 9 6        W       E         ◇ K 7
  ♣ Q 8              S             ♣ J 9 6 5 4
                    ♠ A Q J 10 9 5
                    ♡ 9
                    ◇ A 8 5 2
                    ♣ 10 3
```

After one spade—two clubs some would rebid two diamonds,
and some two spades, which I certainly prefer. Either way,
North–South will finish in four spades. West leads the king of
hearts and plays a second round, which South ruffs.

'When I found the trumps 4–1 I had to take a view in diamonds',
said the first player. 'As West held the long spades I played him for
the short diamonds, leading a low one from hand. East won with the
king and played another heart, forcing my last trump, so when I lost
the third round of diamonds to West he had a heart to cash. One
down.'

'It was much the same at my table', said the second player, and
they passed on to the next board.

My own scoresheet showed +620. I had been dummy and had not paid particular attention to the play. Thinking back, I realised the difference. When my partner ruffed the second heart he immediately played ace and another diamond. East won and led a third heart, reducing the declarer to four trumps. This was the position:

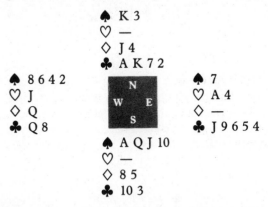

```
              ♠ K 3
              ♡ —
              ◇ J 4
              ♣ A K 7 2
  ♠ 8 6 4 2      N        ♠ 7
  ♡ J        W       E    ♡ A 4
  ◇ Q            S        ◇ —
  ♣ Q 8                   ♣ J 9 6 5 4
              ♠ A Q J 10
              ♡ —
              ◇ 8 5
              ♣ 10 3
```

South gave West his diamond trick and that was the end of the story. If West leads a heart, declarer can ruff in dummy and make the rest.

This was one of the occasions, you see, when it is right to develop the side suit before touching trumps. Even one round of trumps could be a mistake, as declarer might then lack communication after ruffing the fourth heart in dummy. My partner's line was certainly right at any form of aggregate or IMP scoring. In a pairs? Well, then I suppose it would be right to play for the overtrick, drawing trumps and hoping to lose only one diamond trick.

64

Quick Work

An unexpected double of a slam contract, as everybody knows, invites an unexpected lead: generally, not a trump and not the unbid suit. But when there has been a conventional opening bid, such as two clubs, does this count as an unbid suit? Are you warned not to lead a club? East-West had a calamitous misunderstanding on this deal from a Swiss tournament:

```
               Dealer West   Game all
                    ♠ A Q J 10 9 8
                    ♡ A K 10 7 6 3
                    ◇ 9
                    ♣ —
    ♠ K 6 5 4                          ♠ 3 2
    ♡ J 5                              ♡ Q 9 8 2
    ◇ 5 4                              ◇ 10 2
    ♣ Q 10 7 6 5                       ♣ A J 9 8 4
                    ♠ 7
                    ♡ 4
                    ◇ A K Q J 8 7 6 3
                    ♣ K 3 2
```

North-South were playing two clubs Albarran—that is to say, with ace responses. The bidding went as follows:

South	West	North	East
—	No	2♣(1)	No
3◇(2)	No	3♠	No
4NT	No	6♡(3)	No
7NT(4)	No	No	Dble
No	No	No	

(1) It seems a good hand for the system; you will find out at once whether partner holds the ace of diamonds.
(2) Showing just the ace, not the suit.
(3) Well intentioned, but probably unwise.
(4) This was foolish. If partner had held three aces he would doubtless have given the conventional reply.

When East doubled 7NT West thought to himself, 'Neither diamonds nor clubs have been bid naturally, so why should I guess between them? Maybe a spade lead will deter South from finessing?'

But South could see that he would have no chance without a spade finesse. He put in the queen, which held. What should he do now? Demonstrating that his understanding of play was better than his bidding, he claimed the contract!

No doubt, you can see why. There are twelve tricks on top after the spade finesse has held. West is marked with the king of spades and East with the ace of clubs, for it is charitable to assume that if West had held this card he would have led it. So the last four cards will be like this:

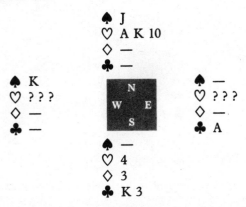

```
              ♠ J
              ♡ A K 10
              ◇ —
              ♣ —
♠ K                        ♠ —
♡ ? ? ?      N             ♡ ? ? ?
◇ —        W   E           ◇ —
♣ —          S             ♣ A
              ♠ —
              ♡ 4
              ◇ 3
              ♣ K 3
```

Even if both defenders hold three hearts, there will be no defence.

65

Snakes and Ladders

In the childhood game of Snakes and Ladders, if I remember correctly, there was a snake just before the winning post that was liable to depose the thrower from 99 to about 30. So I thought the deal below, which cost the North-South pair 1700, would be appropriate at this stage.

Dealer East   Game all

♠ A Q 8 3
♡ 5 3
◇ Q 6 5
♣ K Q J 10

♠ K 4 2
♡ A Q J 8 6 4
◇ A 7
♣ 6 2

♠ —
♡ K 10 9
◇ K J 10 9 4 3
♣ A 9 5 4

♠ J 10 9 7 6 5
♡ 7 2
◇ 8 2
♣ 8 7 3

In a pairs event the bidding at one table went like this:

South	West	North	East
—	—	—	1◇
No	1♡	Dble	2♡
2♠	4♡	No	5♣
No	6♡	No	No
6♠	Dble	No	No
No			

The defence began with two tricks in diamonds, then two in hearts. When East led a third round of diamonds South ruffed with the jack of spades. Following the general principle that it is wrong to overruff when you expect to make the high card in any case, West looked the other way and discarded the 6 of clubs. Now South, placing East with the king of trumps, played a spade to the ace. This left:

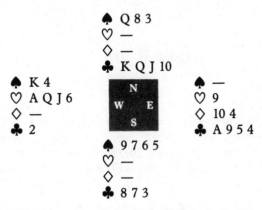

When West came in with the king of spades he led his second club and obtained a club ruff. That was six down, 1700 to the good guys; and a most useful score, because it beat the East–West pairs who played in six hearts and recorded 1460.

66

Lost World

About twenty years ago I made a note of a deal—I think it was in the American *Bridge World*—which seemed to me to contain an interesting theme. I have lost the note, naturally, but I can reconstruct the deal. The North-South hands were something like this:

<pre>
                    ♠ A K 6 3
                    ♡ 7 4
                    ◇ A K Q 5
                    ♣ K 9 5
    ♡ 3 led
                    ♠ 8 7 4
                    ♡ Q 10 9 5 2
                    ◇ 9 6
                    ♣ A 10 8
</pre>

North opens one spade, which is perhaps unusual but hardly a mistake, South responds 1 NT and North raises to 3 NT. West leads the 3 of hearts and East wins with the ace. As you want them to continue hearts, you drop the 5, concealing the 2. East returns the 6 to the 10 and jack; now West advances the queen of clubs.

What will you do on this trick? It is quite possible that West has led from Qx or Qxx, as he can see that there is no future in hearts. In this case the winning play will be to win in dummy, finesse the 10 of clubs, and clear the hearts. But this will be a mistake if the hand is such as:

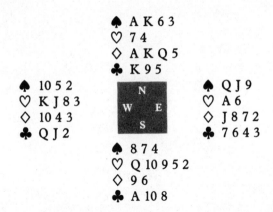

```
              ♠ A K 6 3
              ♡ 7 4
              ◇ A K Q 5
              ♣ K 9 5
♠ 10 5 2          N          ♠ Q J 9
♡ K J 8 3      W     E       ♡ A 6
◇ 10 4 3          S          ◇ J 8 7 2
♣ Q J 2                      ♣ 7 6 4 3
              ♠ 8 7 4
              ♡ Q 10 9 5 2
              ◇ 9 6
              ♣ A 10 8
```

After two hearts, queen of clubs to the king and a club finesse, West will win with the jack of clubs and return a club. Then, even with the spades breaking, you will make only eight tricks.

To win the club return with the ace and finesse on the way back will lose when East holds the jack. I expect you have seen the winning play by now. Play the king of clubs from dummy, overtake with the ace, and knock out the king of hearts. You will have nine sure tricks by way of two spades, two hearts, three diamonds and two clubs. Pretty, isn't it? I wonder how many plays of that sort we all miss in the course of a year.